"There Are Bogart Weeks

for Harvard and Barnard students . . . Bogart Festivals for the film buffs . . . young Bogartians gather round their TV tubes for late late reruns. . . . There are French existentialist critics and American counterparts trying to define the passionate reaction this cool underplayer excites in a new generation young enough to be his grandchildren . . . a complex, hard-working, hard-drinking, outspoken, witty and cynically rebellious and yet strangely Victorian, raucous and intelligent man . . . able to make contact in a special, intuitive way."

—Budd Schulberg,
WASHINGTON POST

HUMPHREY BOGART
was famous in his lifetime and has been a growing legend in the years since his death. Here at last is the only authorized and complete biography of his amazing life.

BOGIE
is the story of a true original, the anti-phony and nearly anti-social screenstar who left an indelible mark upon the world's imagination.

Joe Hyams, former reporter for the *New York Herald Tribune*, is the co-author of *The Weekend Gambler's Handbook* and *My Life with Cleopatra* (with Walter Wanger). His work has appeared in such magazines as *Playboy*, *Saturday Evening Post*, and *McCall's*. Mr. Hyams and his wife, actress Elke Sommer, live in Hollywood.

Other SIGNET Books of Special Interest

☐ **CONVERSATIONS IN THE RAW by Rex Reed.** This may well be the interview's finest hour. Rex Reed has captured his subjects in those off-guard moments when they are most truly themselves. In Conversations In The Raw he interviews Bette Davis as she opens up about her problems with men; Oskar Werner confesses his own superiority; Leslie Caron talks about Warren Beatty; Patty Duke describes her childhood; plus many other exciting interviews. (#Y4289—$1.25)

☐ **DO YOU SLEEP IN THE NUDE? by Rex Reed.** Rex Reed interviews Barbra Streisand, Warren Beatty, Ava Gardner, Mike Nichols, Lester Maddox and many others—and stripping them of their public image, gets down to the truth about their private lives. (#Q3773—95¢)

☐ **ON MAKING A MOVIE: BREWSTER McCLOUD by C. Kirk McClelland.** The day-by-day record of the time McClelland spent closely examining the entire complex technical process and complicated human drama of the creation of Brewster McCloud. It is a non-starry-eyed, irreverent and beautifully incisive revelation of movie-makers at work. (#W4591—$1.50)

☐ **DRAT! W. C. Fields' Picture Book, edited by Richard J. Anobile.** Introduction by Ed McMahon. DRAT is the encapsulate view, and what a view! of the greatest comedian of the century. Here, in happy juxtaposition of photos and quotes, is the irreverent irrelevancy of W. C. Fields, the man and the actor. (#Q3933—95¢)

BOGIE

The Biography of *HUMPHREY BOGART*

By JOE HYAMS

Introduction by LAUREN BACALL

A SIGNET BOOK

NEW AMERICAN LIBRARY

TIMES MIRROR

For my wife Elke, who never knew Bogie, and for Betty, who knew him better than anyone.

Introduction

Bogie used to say rather wistfully that as a kid he always felt a bit cheated that because he was born on Christmas Day he never had a birthday. And now he has one every day.

There is not a good friend or acquaintance of Humphrey Bogart's whose life was not better for having known him and whose life is now less good because he's not around.

There are few people in one's life that leave much of a mark—a lasting one. Bogie surely did and, remarkably, Bogie does. No one who knew him, even a little, could forget him—neither could those who never knew him at all. And no one would ever want to. One had to recognize his respect for human dignity—the balloons he pricked were always overblown. He was able to cope with the world he lived in, no matter what it was, because of his purity of thought. He is the only man I have ever known who truly and completely belonged to himself. That was one of his major attractions for other men, I think. In the motion picture business—the goldfish bowl as he called it, in which he lived with all the temptations and attractions of easy, high living; the acceptance of glamor as reality; the shading of the truth—he had absolute clarity of purpose. His friends, the most talented and intelligent of them, were in awe of his concepts. "How did he do it at all and how did he do it without being a bore, without sacrificing his wit, humor, his magic as a man?" He did it because his convictions about life, work and people were so strong they were unshakable. Nothing—no one—could make him lower his standards, lessen his character.

Character, a trait rare in our world today, was to Bogie the most treasured thing a man could have. He felt that if you thought a wrong thought—though no one else knew—the fact that you knew was enough to affect and damage that character. The result being that you are worth less to yourself and to your world. Extreme yes—but the best kind of extreme. He used to say, "You pays your money and you takes your choice." He did both.

He recognized the imperfections of life and people. He accepted them, lived with them but was not embittered by them. He learned at an early age that the extras that were to be had in life were worked for. Nobody ever gave Bogie anything. Whatever he finally had in a material way, he earned. It was a constant revelation to me and uplifting to my spirit that Bogie was not soured or bitter about his own life and the many sadnesses that he faced beginning with his young manhood.

He never tried to be popular. He gave greatly in friendship and expected little or at least was aware of the limits of his friends and accepted them as they were, not as he hoped they would be. He was in fact surprised that the motion picture industry was so genuinely happy when he won the Oscar and surprised at the concern of so many when he first became ill.

He had incredible understanding of and patience with all people, especially with me. He was a partaker of life, a man of class—true class— a career, a respecter, a protector. "Home flourishes on care," he said, "not neglect." He never neglected it and it flourished. Home was precious to him and the people in it inviolable. Honor was basic. He simply would not accept a lie—not from me, a friend, or his children. He was a romantic, an idealist, a gallant man—always on the alert for something better.

I think of the many who came into our house that last year of his life. They wanted to be in his presence to reassure themselves that he was still there—with his wit, his warmth, his substance, and his barbs as well—that Bogart was indestructible. None would have thought, certainly he would not, that in the greater sense he was indestructible. Today, nine years after his death, he lives—more vital than ever, even more affecting, not only to new generations, but to his own and to me. There have been many men conscious of history—wanting so to leave their mark to be remembered, men of great position on a world level. Bogie was not one of these men, he didn't think that way. And yet he has left more than most men ever do. His spirit, courage, truth, and character will live as long as a scrap of film remains intact. He had the greatest gifts a man could have: respect for himself, for his craft, for all people—integrity about life as well as work. He couldn't let anyone else down; he would be letting himself down and he had to live with himself.

Is it any wonder his presence is felt more now than ever? One could not see him in a film and forget; one could not know him or see him and not feel the bigness of him and have some of that character rub off—one could not know him or see him and not be richer. As we frantically search in our various worlds for some kind of answer, here is something to hang on to—someone to feel safer because of. As I look back on my own life and think of the men I have known—a few great, many famed, some of genius—Bogie stands out as a giant. And not because he tried to be. But because he was. He had the great gift of communication with all people, of all ages, in all walks of life; so he left all who knew him even slightly, poorer with his loss. The thousands of letters that were written to me upon the news of his death: it affected cab drivers, housewives, gardeners, cooks, any and all who had seen him on the screen and strangely felt a part of him. His effect on his friends who held dearly to every moment of laughter and foolishness. A practical joke became a precious moment. But the most rewarding and exciting and warming thing to me is that now all those people, all of us, have again in the palms of our hands and in our hearts those moments to muse and laugh over, moments that involved this most unique man. He would have been pleased by the recognition of new generations. They involve his own children.

There is hardly a day that passes that I don't remember something he said to me. He used to say, "Long after I'm gone you'll remember this." And I do. I remember it all. If there was one thing about Bogie that infuriated me it was that in the final analysis he was always right. That is not to say that he was self-righteous or that his life was lived without mistakes—there were certainly those—but the main road was straight at all times and as he would see me start to wander off at odd moments he would gently and subtly pull me back until my direction was finally as clear as his and as straight. His sights were high.

And I must quite candidly say that there were moments when I felt a tinge of jealousy. Those were the moments when Bogie talked of his boat. She was trim, sleek, pure, beautiful, and she sailed the open seas, the last free place on earth. In addition, unlike a woman, she never talked back. That reminds me of a funny and marvelous and half-serious idea that Bogie expressed. A woman should be small enough to fit into a man's pocket, so that when he was in the mood to see her he could put her in the palm of his hand, allow her to dance and smile and even speak, but when she began to go too far, back in the pocket she would go. I am laughing as I write it; an infuriating, imaginative and enchanting notion. Now back to the sea. How his face would light up at the thought of it—the joy the ocean and sailing brought him. That was his place, his health, his sanity. That was my greatest competitor and thank God he had it.

I find it difficult to write about him. Not because of a lack of ideas but perhaps because of too many. My head is so full of vivid pictures, words he spoke—gifts I received from him that are helping me still in my constant contact with life's abrasions. He left me with a sense of laughter—a sense that in spite of the worst possible adversity there still could conceivably be something to laugh about. He was my husband, my teacher, my friend. He was a vulnerable, humorous man, too easily touched by people, resourceful, thoughtful, disciplined, hungry for knowledge—improvement in every conceivable way; never a bystander, a disinterested party. He was tremendously proud of being an actor—a good one. He fiercely resented members of his profession who did not take their work seriously and producers and directors to whom the word "actor" was an epithet. Bogie was a pushover—a soft touch—sentimental, loving and a giver. He is still giving. He was a man to whom personal happiness and success came late—but that it came at all was his proof that he had not believed in vain. He had to fight for every good part he ever had, but in spite of that he never lost faith.

He had no religion in the accepted social sense, but he was the most religious man I have ever known. He believed in the Ten Commandments and the Golden Rule and he lived by them uncompromisingly. He took a great deal of me with him when he went, but he left the rest of me stronger. For all of it I shall always be grateful. I was the most privileged and the luckiest of women.

Many people have written many words about Bogie—some friends, some pseudo-friends. I write about him as a man who shaped my life—who from the beginning saw to it that I never lost sight of myself or lost humor about myself—who in my first flush of acclaim kept my feet firmly on the ground—who taught me that whatever laudatory remarks were made about me in columns were not to be taken too seriously as they were mostly plants by the studio star makers.

He was a man who made it possible for me to survive after he was gone—who made it possible to play the game of life with him to the end. He always said that when he died he wanted no mourning for him. He believed those who mourned for the dead were really mourning for themselves. He wanted friends to drink a private toast and have a laugh. And that is what they did.

He gave me an appreciation of life—life lived and shared with someone. He taught me that we all chose our way of life and no matter what direction the lives of our friends might take—however attractive or romantic they might seem—we must never lose sight of our own. He showed me that liking between men and women was the most lasting thing, the most valued. We liked each other. And to paraphrase a quote of Joe Hyams that Bogie said about our son, Steve—"I loved him—I hope he knew that."

New York
April, 1966

Lauren Bacall

ONE

Bogie was the bravest man I have ever met. And that includes a lot of unknown heroes who were my friends in the South Pacific during World War II—during those days when I formulated my personal belief that the final test of a man is the way he faces death. Bogie faced death the way he faced life: with courage and dignity as a gentleman.

It was no secret in Hollywood that Bogie was dying of cancer. But it is a curious fact that until news of this sort leaks out in public a man's privacy is respected. Bogie knew that and he knew that if it were generally known how sick he was, the press would soon have a deathwatch on his house. Cameramen with long lenses and news reporters with keen eyes would be waiting to be first with the pictures and the story.

So he battled alone bravely, and those of us who knew and loved him and had respected his right to live as he wanted also respected his right to die the way he wanted.

And he made it easy for us. If he was as conscious of the imminence of death as I am sure he must have been, he never mentioned it, never allowed its presence to cloud what might be a last visit or a last interview. Brave as he was, his wife, Lauren Bacall, whom he called Betty, was his equal in gallantry.

As the newspaperman closest to him for the last decade of his life, and the only one whom he saw regularly during the last year and hours of his life, I was privy to the terrible drama that preceded his death. I will never forget one of those last days when he was being prepared to receive company at the cocktail hour. He was little more than a genial skeleton by then, lying most of the time in the upstairs bedroom of the Bogart home in Holmby Hills.

He lay on the bed, head propped on pillows, and helplessly submitted to the nurses who attended him around the clock. On that afternoon a fat nurse cushioned his head gently and began to lather his face.

"There now, Mr. Bogart," she said, drawing back for a better look at her razor work. "We look just fine." She held a little vanity mirror of Betty's to his face. He nodded and rubbed his right hand over his jaw slowly, reflectively. It was an old habit, started when the doctors dug a wood splinter out of his lip in the First World War.

Betty came into the bedroom, carrying the old Daks bought in London and the scarlet smoking jacket she had given him last Christmas-birthday. She put the trousers on, right leg first, then the left leg, and then pulled them up over his waist. They were loose.

"Christ, I'm going to have to gain some weight," he said.

"Harry Cohn is having the script rewritten for you," Betty said.

"I always claimed he was a bastard," he said. "Maybe I ought to start changing my mind."

"Why?" said Betty. "He just wants you in the picture. He figures you're worth waiting for, but he's still a bastard."

"The hell with that picture," he said. "What about the boat? How're they doing on the hull?"

"Pete says it'll be ready by the weekend," she said.

He nodded, then winced with pain. Aurilio, the handyman, and the nurse picked him up out of the bed and lifted him into the wheelchair.

He pushed the wheelchair himself to the dumbwaiter shaft across the room, seeming proud that he still had the strength to propel it. For a moment it looked as if he would try to get out of the chair and walk, but then he gave it up.

They lifted him out of the chair and sat him on a little stool in the dumbwaiter shaft. The top had been removed to give him headroom. "Are you all right, Mr. Bogart?" the nurse asked.

"Yeah, just dandy," he said, making the words sound cheerful and sarcastic at the same time. Down below in the kitchen Aurilio was pulling the ropes. The little elevator started slowly down.

It was dark in the shaft and the ride from bedroom to kitchen was less than twenty seconds, but he obviously hated it. They lifted him out of the dumbwaiter shaft and back into the wheelchair, in which he was transported through the house: a fourteen-room house, with a four-car garage, a tennis court, a swimming pool, and an acre of lawn. Taxes on the house alone higher than most people's incomes. Four servants, three dogs, two children.

The marble floor of the patio facing the pool was polished to a high gloss. He put his hands on the chair wheels and brought it to a halt, examining the pool house intently. "It's off center," he said. "Fifteen thousand dollars and they can't even follow a plumb line."

The little group following him in the chair looked like a tableau from *Sunset Boulevard*. He rolled past the living room, which was rarely used. Everything in the room was expensive: from the Dufys and the Picassos to the French Provincial furniture. They had spent a quarter of a million dollars on the room and it still wasn't finished. Betty was going to have the first big party in it when he was well.

A huge boxer dog came running in and jumped up almost on his lap. "Get down, Harvey," Bogie said gruffly, meanwhile patting him gently on the head.

In the library he wheeled to his chair opposite the bar. They sat him down, smoothed out his trousers, and gave him his props—a watered-down martini for the left hand, a cigarette for the right. It was a few minutes after five, and he said his back already hurt like hell.

"How're you feeling otherwise?" I asked.

"You can say I'm down to my last martini," Bogie said. "But I'm fighting to keep my head above the press."

The library telephone rang. Betty came quietly into the room, moving like a leopard. She picked up the phone, listened a minute, then said, "Nonsense, Bogie is fine."

"Here, let me talk," he said and got on the extension phone on the table next to him. "I'm getting along well, just a little underweight," he said, putting his hand over the telephone while he coughed.

"This is an old rumor. Last time you people had me on the eighth floor of the Los Angeles Memorial Hospital. The fact that there is no such hospital doesn't bother me, but the eighth floor is what burned me. That's pretty ominous sounding, isn't it? You can tell your bosses I'm fine, never felt better."

He banged the phone into its cradle. Another coughing spasm was interrupted by the phone again. He reached for it. It was an editor calling to check for himself on whether a reporter had really talked with Bogart.

He was furious. "You don't trust your reporters, then fire them. What kind of newspaper are you running? I'm going to call my lawyer to see what legal action we can take against you people printing that I was in a coma. Then you'll know you talked with me."

This time when he hung up there was a thin smile on his face. "What's the matter with you newspapermen?" he said. "Don't you ever check stories?"

I recognized the familiar needling technique and started to fiddle with my pipe.

"Well, aren't you sometimes ashamed of your profession?" Bogie persisted.

"Aren't you sometimes ashamed of being an actor when you read a fan magazine?" I asked.

Bogie grinned broadly and settled back in the chair as Betty brought me a Coke.

"I didn't ask you to come here to freeload on my whiskey," Bogie said, and reached for a statement he had dictated the day before. Waving it in front of me, he asked, "Will you promise to print this exactly as written?"

It was a difficult promise to give. As the only reporter who saw Bogie regularly, I had written almost every story published about him since his illness began. As a friend I felt I had an obligation to help keep his spirits up, but as a reporter I had an obligation to tell the truth.

Usually I flavored the truth with humor, as I had in the story written before Bogie had gone to the hospital on October 8, 1956. I had told my editors the truth then: I suspected he was dying of cancer but I didn't want us to break the story. Once it came out authoritatively that he was dying, the press would set a deathwatch by his door—reporters by the score and TV cameras, all vying to be first with the obituary. A grisly business.

But I figured I could agree to print the story as he wanted it—as long as I could preface it with an introduction. Bogie said he didn't care how I introduced the story as long as I ran it as written. He handed me a carbon of a neatly typed, single-spaced letter and read aloud from the original in a hoarse voice, occasionally racked by coughing.

An open letter to the working press:

I have been greatly disturbed lately at the many un-checked and baseless rumors being tossed among you regarding the state of my health. Just to set the record straight, as they say in Washington (and I have as much right to say this as anybody in Washington has), a great deal of what has been printed has had nothing to do with the true facts. It may be even necessary for me to send out a truth team to follow you all around.

I have read that both lungs have been removed, that I couldn't live for another half hour, that I was fighting for my life in some hospital which doesn't exist out here, that my heart had been removed and replaced by an old gasoline pump salvaged from a defunct Standard Oil station. I have been on the way to practically every cemetery, you name 'em, from here to the Mississippi including several where I'm certain they only accept dogs. All the above upsets my friends, not to mention the insurance companies—so, as they also say in Washington, let's get the facts to the American people—and here they are.

I had a slight malignancy in the esophagus. So that some of you won't have to go to the research depart-ment, it's the pipe that runs from your throat to your stomach. The operation for the removal of the malig-nancy was successful, although it was touch-and-go for a while whether the malignancy or I would survive.

As they also say in Washington, I'm a better man than I ever was and all I need now is about thirty pounds in weight, which I'm sure some of you could spare. Possibly we could start something like a Weight Bank for Bogart, and, believe me, I'm not particular from which portion of your anatomies it comes from.

In closing, any time you want to run a little medical bulletin on me, just pick up the phone, and as they say in the old country, I'm in the book!

"You promised," Bogie said when he finished the letter. "Now keep your word and don't change a word or I'll nomi-nate you for membership in the rat pack."

Bogie tilted his drink gently on his lips and savored the taste on his tongue. "Here's to Mark Twain. Reports of his death were exaggerated too."

The doorbell started ringing and other friends began to

arrive: David Niven, Frank Sinatra, Spencer Tracy, George Cukor, Katherine Hepburn, Richard Burton. The guests settled down in the casual way of people who know each other well, see each other often.

The conversation was directed at him and made for him. He knew it and loved it. If he couldn't go out, his world came to him. It had been this way for months. The list he kept of the people who had phoned or come to see him during the time he was sick almost filled a small notebook.

Only a few were conspicuous by their absences. But Bogie understood. "They're afraid of death and they don't want to be reminded of it," he once explained to Betty.

Betty felt differently. She was angry at the ones who stayed away. He tried to make her understand: He didn't like to be around sick people himself. It depressed him, not because he was afraid of death but because he loved life so much. But he couldn't convince her.

His hand went automatically to his chin, as it always did when he was thinking, and he looked at all the people in the room with him. "Funny," he said to me quietly, "I never considered myself particularly well liked. I really never knew before just how many friends I do have."

Betty was the perfect hostess in the perfect setting, talking and laughing with the guests but always with an eye on her husband to see that he was comfortable, to see that he was included in the conversation.

"Class, that's what she has—real class," Bogie had once said, and he'd told me about the night he suggested she go out with the gang, feeling she must have been bored with staying at home with him night after night. He didn't want her to say yes, but he felt he should make the suggestion and tried to make it sound as though he meant it.

"I don't want to go any place without you. That's not why I married you," she said.

"A lot of broads in this town, but I married a real lady with class," he'd told me proudly.

The crowd started to leave, one by one. He was still in the chair, cigarette in hand and a glass half full, when the door shut for the last time and the routine that brought him to the room was reversed. Once more he was in the dumbwaiter shaft being hauled up to the bedroom and undressed by Betty and Aurilio. It was good to lie down. He was tired, but his thoughts roamed restlessly. Although the body was weakened from pain and illness, his mind seemed more alive than ever.

Stephen came into the room to say good night, wearing pajamas and a terry robe. Seven, and very much the young man, he hugged his father and giggled.

"What's so funny?" Bogie asked.

"I was thinking of the day you took me to Romanoff's," Steve said.

The incident had taken place shortly before Bogie had become ill. He decided one day that Stephen should take his place in the world of men.

Betty dressed Stephen up in new long trousers and brought him in for a critical once-over. They went off together—father and son on an outing—and got into the Jag. First stop was Romanoff's, where they went to the booth by the door that was always reserved for him.

Mike visited them and then the gang came by. Bogie had a martini with everyone who stopped to admire his son. By the fifth drink Stephen got a little restless and began pounding the glasses with his fork.

When they got home they weren't speaking. Betty asked Bogie how it went. "Never again," he said, echoed by Stephen, who said, "You bet."

"Good night, Stephen," Bogie said and settled his head on the pillows.

Outside it was dark. I heard the creak of trees rubbing against the house. Wind from the east, I thought, about fifteen knots. I thought of the *Santana* floating gently at Catalina, her hull newly painted, waiting for him.

TWO

One night some years ago Humphrey Bogart expounded on the subject of "class" before a gathering of the Hollywood elite. Sid Luft, husband of Judy Garland, had just purchased a Rolls-Royce. That item of conspicuous consumption, along with bench-made English shoes and a butler who doubled as chauffeur, spelled class to Luft. Then Bogart took the floor. In a voice honed with sarcasm he announced, "You can't buy it and you can't acquire it like a suntan. And I can tell you that you don't have it, my friend, and you never will. I know what I'm talking about because I was born with it. I've had it all my life—and I can also do without it."

Bogart had threaded his needle with truth and his friends knew it. The statement that he was "born with class" was a fact, although a good part of the time one would never have suspected that he had been brought up in an old and socially prominent family.

But the Bogart family is included in each edition of *Dau's New York Blue Book,* from its first publication in 1907 until it was discontinued three decades later. And in those years society was Society indeed: Dr. Belmont DeForest Bogart, Humphrey's father, was a third-generation American who could trace his family's ancestry back to 1500 through a long line of respectable Dutch burghers.

Bogart's mother, Maude Humphrey, was also a third-generation American. She had studied art in Paris under Whistler. By the time she was thirty she had become one of the most famous magazine illustrators in America.

They were a handsome couple. Dr. Bogart was tall, slim, and well built. He was a natural athlete, an expert at most sports, and a superb wing shot. Miss Humphrey, who was almost his height, was redheaded and attractive, with an imposing carriage and elegant manners. She had an incisive wit that discouraged many suitors but delighted her young husband. He too had a sharp tongue, and a chronic family problem was finding servants who would tolerate his blistering sarcasm.

The Bogarts married relatively late—she was thirty-three and he was thirty-four—after a long courtship that began while he was still a student at Columbia College of Physicians and Surgeons in Manhattan. He graduated in 1896 and was licensed to practice medicine the following year. In 1898, after he was established, he and Miss Humphrey were wed.

They were both politically conservative. He was a Republican and Presbyterian. She was a Tory and Episcopalian. Miss Humphrey was, in addition, a leader in the early suffragette movement. She believed strongly in equal rights for women, not only at the polls but in the home.

Those were the days when an income tax was unthinkable, when John Jacob Astor could say, "A man who has a million dollars is as well-off as if he were rich." The Bogarts were not rich by comparison with Mr. Astor, but they were rich by any ordinary standards. Miss Humphrey earned as much as $40,000 a year illustrating stories for such publications as the *Delineator* and painting advertisements and magazine covers. Dr. Bogart inherited money from his father, who had invented a process of lithographing on tin, and, in addition, averaged $20,000 a year from his practice.

Their combined income enabled them to live very well, particularly when one considers that in those days a couple could get a mahogany parlor table for $3.95, a brass-trimmed bed for $3.00, a sofa for $9.98. Corned beef sold for eight cents a pound and a good suit cost $10.65. The Bogarts had four servants: a cook at $5 a week, a laundress for $3.50 a week, and two maids at $3.50 a week apiece.

Their home, a four-story, limestone house with bay windows and heavy decorations in bas-relief, was at 245 West 103rd Street, near Riverside Drive. At the turn of the century that area was a very fashionable thoroughfare, lined with upper-class residences and the kind of shops that are now called boutiques. The Bogart home was across the street from the old Hotel Marseilles, an elegant residential hotel that boasted among its permanent residents Sara Delano Roosevelt, FDR's mother, and the wealthy Rheingold Beer brothers.

Dr. Bogart conducted his medical practice from a mahogany-paneled office on the first floor. Because he was a doctor, the Bogarts were one of the few families in their block with a telephone. The house was heavy with tapestries, urns, velvet hangings, potted palms, carved ceilings, rubber plants, and classical statues holding light fixtures with alabaster shades. The parquet floors were covered with Oriental rugs. The family also boasted a Gramophone, complete with horn, and recordings of Caruso and dialect comedians on cylindrical wax records kept wrapped in cotton in small cartons.

In December, 1899, Mrs. Bogart was in her ninth month of pregnancy. The household was in the tumult customary at such times, as Mrs. Bogart busied herself with assembling a layette and decorating the baby's nursery—blue, because both she and the doctor wanted a boy.

The day before Christmas Mrs. Bogart went to the Keppel Gallery in midtown Manhattan, against the advice of her husband, to see a display of original drawings of the Gibson Girl. On Christmas Eve she complained of pains, which Dr. Bogart at first attributed to overexertion. But soon she was unmistakably in labor and he rushed outside to hail a hansom cab.

It was a wet, cold night with a light snow falling, and it took some time for the doctor and his anxious wife to get from their home to Sloan's Maternity Hospital in upper Manhattan. A few hours later, Mrs. Bogart gave birth to an eight-pound-seven-ounce son—on Christmas Day, a fact Humphrey later lamented: "I never had a birthday of my own to celebrate," he used to complain, "I got cheated out of a birthday."

The Bogarts had often discussed a name for their firstborn if he was a boy. Mrs. Bogart persuaded her husband that he be named Humphrey after her, but as a concession to him the child was given the middle name of DeForest.

One night, when Humphrey was only a few months old, Dr. Bogart proudly told friends over cigars and port after dinner at Luchow's Restaurant that it was obvious from his son's firm grip that he would be a surgeon. The doctor took to stopping other physicians in the corridors at Presbyterian Hospital, where he was a heart and lungs specialist, to ask whether they thought Columbia or Yale was the better college for a future surgeon. It was soon decided between himself and Mrs. Bogart that young Humphrey would go to Yale.

The new baby occasioned little change in the family's routine. Dr. Bogart held his office hours downstairs while his wife worked in an upstairs studio with a skylight. It was here that behind her locked door she frequently endured anguishing migraine headaches.

Humphrey's airings were usually the responsibility of a young Irish nurse who took him out in a high-wheeled carriage, but one afternoon, Mrs. Bogart herself took Humphrey to Central Park. While the baby was playing in his carriage she made a sketch of him. When they returned home, she worked over the sketch and sent it off to an advertising agency. It was bought by Mellins Baby Food for use in their ads and on their labels. It soon became the most popular baby picture of the day and made the infant Humphrey famous as the "Original Maude Humphrey Baby."

Each summer the Bogarts, like other well-to-do New York families, went through an elaborate ritual of departure for their summer home—in their case at Canandaigua Lake, one of New York's Finger Lakes. First the city house was thoroughly cleaned, a process that took days. On the day before departure the expressman and his big wagon called for the trunks. On the tumultuous morning of departure the family and servants assembled a mountain of bags, coats, umbrellas, and sports gear, and proceeded to the railroad station in two or three horse-drawn cabs.

When Humphrey was two years old the ritual was interrupted as the family was proceeding by Pullman car to their summer home. Mrs. Bogart, who was pregnant again, announced she was in labor. Dr. Bogart and his wife got off the train and found room in a boardinghouse, where the doctor himself delivered his wife of a daughter, who was christened Frances. The following year at about the same time Mrs. Bogart gave birth to another daughter, Catherine Elizabeth, in Presbyterian Hospital.

Shortly after Frances was born, Humphrey became seriously ill with pneumonia. Thereafter, his mother was never quite convinced that he was not a sickly child. She wrote a friend about this time, "He is a manly lad, but too delicate in health." Indeed, that concern is about as close as Bogart's mother came to showing maternal emotion.

"I was brought up very unsentimentally but very straight-forwardly," Bogart once said. "A kiss, in our family, was an event. Our mother and father didn't glug over my two sisters and me. They had too many things to do, and so did we. Anyway, we were mainly the responsibility of the servants.

"I can't say that I loved my mother, but I respected her. Ours was not the kind of affection that spills over or makes pretty pictures. If, when I was grown up, I sent my mother one of those Mother's Day telegrams or said it with flowers, she would have returned the wire and flowers to me, collect."

He also remembered that his mother and father used to have terrible fights. "We kids would pull the covers over our ears to keep out the sound of fighting," he said. "Our home was kept together for the sake of the children as well as for the sake of propriety."

The arguments usually stemmed from one source—money. Dr. Bogart preferred hunting, fishing, and sailing to medicine. More and more the responsibility for the family finances rested on Mrs. Bogart.

"My father liked to get away from his patients into the open air," Bogart said. "It was a good way for me to dodge any prissying up around the house. We went sailing, hunting, and fishing together."

By the time he was eight, young Humphrey was an expert at sailing his own Great South Bay One Designer sloop at Lake Canandaigua.

When not quite fourteen, Humphrey was enrolled at Trinity School, an old and select Episcopal institution for young gentlemen located on 91st Street near Amsterdam Avenue. First, he visited Brooks (forerunner of Brooks Brothers), which was then located on Broadway near 22nd Street. There he was outfitted in the proper school attire: blue-serge suit, including vest, white shirts with detachable collars, held on fore and aft by brass buttons, and a Chesterfield overcoat with fly front and black-velvet collar for winter wear.

Trinity was run along the lines of a British boys' school. The day started at 9 A.M. with services in the chapel. Latin, Greek, and German were prominent in the curriculum, and there was a high premium on memorization of almost everything.

The head of the school, the rector, was Lawrence T. Cole,

affectionately called Bunny Cole. A beneficent and compassionate gentleman, the rector always wore a black cassock tied around his waist with a tasseled cord.

Years later Bogart was to recall one of many sessions in the rector's study.

"Herr Luther has reported you again," the headmaster said.

"Yes, sir."

"He complains that you started a riot in class this morning, and he's given you a failure in German."

"Yes, sir."

"Why?"

"I don't like German."

"Nor Herr Luther?"

"No, sir."

"Since you don't like German and you don't like English or history or economics, will you tell me if there's anything you do like, Master Bogart?"

"I like math, sir. Algebra."

"Why?"

"Because there's nothing theoretical about it—it's simply fact. You can do a problem and get your answer and then you prove the answer's right."

"But these riots! This endless flaunting of all authority. Why do you do these things?"

Humphrey didn't have an answer to that question then, though years later he was to volunteer one: "I always liked stirring up things, needling authority. Even in my childhood it gave me pleasure. I guess I inherited it from my parents. They needled everyone, including each other."

Humphrey's attendance at Trinity is still remembered by his classmates. Eric Hodgins, the writer, recalls that Humphrey wore a black derby hat day in and day out. "That made him a standout in the class," says Mr. Hodgins, who never did figure out what significance the strange headgear had for young Humphrey.

"He was not a loner, and it was obvious from the way that Humphrey bore himself that he belonged to an 'in' group in school—though just what group was never clear," Mr. Hodgins says. "He was friendly but a bit distant— what would be described today as 'playing it cool.' "

Humphrey's closest friend was not a Trinity classmate. He was William A. Brady, Jr., son of a next-door neighbor who had come to see Dr. Bogart complaining of a touch of pto-

maine, that Victorian term used to cover diseases ranging
from indigestion to a heart attack.

Mr. Brady, Sr., was a fascinating man who had managed
Gentleman Jim Corbett and Jim Jeffries, the heavyweight
champion. Before his wife, actress Grace George, agreed to
marry him, he had had to promise to quit promoting prize-
fights. His new dream was to step into the theatrical producing class of David Belasco.

A big, handsome man, William A. Brady had been married
before and had a daughter half a generation older than
Humphrey named Alice. Bill, Jr., his son with Miss George,
was Humphrey's age. The two boys became good friends.

Every Saturday afternoon they would go on passes given
them by Mr. Brady to one of the Broadway shows. In later
years, when Humphrey was famous, he said that his notion of
great acting came from these expeditions. By the time he was
thirteen he had seen Laurette Taylor in *Peg O' My Heart*,
Maude Adams as Peter Pan, Nazimova in *Bella Donna*. He
recalled having seen Sarah Bernhardt at the Palace Theater
in a vaudeville act that featured in third place a comic jug-
gler named W. C. Fields.

With young Bill Brady he saw moving pictures at Brooklyn's Orpheum Theater that offered photographed bits of famous stage acts including Alice Lloyd, Eva Tanguay, and
James J. Morton. And they saw one of America's first color
pictures, a 700-foot Kinemacolor feature starring Willie Collier, Raymond Hitchcock, and Anna Held.

Although Bill's father was in show business, it was on a
gentlemanly level. Like all proper people, the Bogarts were
scornful of public entertainers who thrived on the attentions
of the press. Dr. Bogart once repeated to Humphrey the
adage that there were only three times a gentleman's name
appeared in the papers—when he was born, when he was
married, and when he died. Of course, one could glow quietly over certain kinds of publicity. For example, when Humphrey was ten years old, Dr. Bogart handed him a heavy,
leather-bound volume. "Look through this for a familiar
name," the doctor said. Humphrey found that his father had
been given several paragraphs in *Who's Who in New York*.

"My father was very proud," Bogart later recalled, "but I
think my mother was miffed. Her name wasn't in it."

Humphrey was raised to be a very proper young man. In
white-kid gloves and patent-leather pumps he danced at cotil-
lions with young ladies of whom his parents approved. In

those days at Trinity a lady's man was referred to as a "fusser." Although Humphrey did not win acclaim as the biggest "fusser" in his class, Mr. Hodgins remembers him as a contender for the title.

During the summer when he was fifteen, Humphrey fell in love for the first time—with a girl named Pickles. The First World War was in full swing and it was the year of the Scares: the U-Boat Scare and the Infantile Paralysis Scare, the second of which quarantined the Bogart family on Fire Island for two months. It was their first season on the island —every other year they had spent the summers at Lake Canandaigua.

Humphrey complained bitterly to his parents when they decided to vacation nearer home. He complained, that is, until he met Pickles. Then, since he was fifteen and the circumstances were right, he fell in love. He recalled her as having "laughing eyes, and freckles on her nose—and there was a sense of drama about it all—we were quarantined, and who knew when we would get off the island."

But one moonlit night they pledged their troth with a couple of hot dogs, sealed it with a mustard-flavored kiss, and said good-bye. The quarantine had been lifted.

A photograph taken that summer shows Humphrey sitting on the running board of what appears to be a Stutz Bearcat, a Pekingese dog in his arms and a pipe in his hand. He looked every inch the F. Scott Fitzgerald prototype—even to the hair parted carefully in the middle and slicked down.

Back in Manhattan once more, young Humphrey mooned about the house until Pickles wrote and invited him to visit her. She lived in Flatbush. The trip from Manhattan took him two and one half hours each way. He made it just once, love for Pickles dying rapidly as the realization of what romance could cost in terms of travel and expense was borne in upon him.

By the next summer at Fire Island Pickles was forgotten. This time Humphrey lost his heart to a sweet-voiced, dark-haired little charmer named Bonnie Bremler, but she lived in Montclair, New Jersey, which is considerably farther from New York than Flatbush. Again he bravely made one trip to see his summer love, but this time he was prepared—he took along a package of sandwiches for the ride and did not arrange another meeting.

Meanwhile, with all the other students at Trinity, Humphrey was hell-bent to get into the army. While he impatiently waited to become old enough to enlist, he faithfully did his part by such unromantic work as collecting peach pits. These were used for activated charcoal in gas masks.

The war was responsible for young Humphrey's interest in guns. His first real weapon was a Daisy Air Rifle given him as a present on his thirteenth Christmas-birthday. He soon learned to dismantle it, and with stock and barrel artfully concealed in his pant leg, he would stiff-leggedly leave his house of an evening to meet young Bill Brady.

Together the boys would walk—Humphrey favoring the gimpy leg—to a construction site on Riverside Drive. Here they would put the gun together and shoot the globes out of the red lanterns.

In time, the boys managed to acquire a .22 pistol. One night they were careless and the pistol went off. The bullet went through Humphrey's wrist, fortunately without doing any serious damage.

The boys had sufficient presence of mind to smash an electric light bulb on the floor as an alibi in case anybody heard the shot. Bill fled guiltily to the Hudson River, where he dumped the revolver. Then he and Humphrey went to a doctor who patched up the wrist. The doctor, however, notified Dr. Bogart, who decided that this incident indicated it was high time his son went away to the preparatory school he himself had attended, Phillips Academy at Andover, Massachusetts, to prepare for Yale.

On January 30, 1917, Dr. Bogart wrote a letter to Dr. Alfred E. Stearns, the academy's distinguished headmaster.

"I am anxious to send my boy of seventeen years, now at Trinity School in this city, to Andover next year," he wrote. "Will you kindly send catalogue concerning the school expenses, board, etc. As I have other children to consider it will be necessary to limit his expenses as much as possible.

"You will remember me as your teammate in baseball, also football, class of 1888. . . ."

But Humphrey was not finished at Trinity. He had to repeat his third year's studies. Just before college board exams he came down with scarlet fever. Bunny Cole assembled all of Humphrey's classmates and others who had physical contact with him to say in solemn tones that the entire class was quarantined.

By the end of summer Humphrey was well again and had been accepted at Andover. On September 12, 1917, Dr. Bogart wrote to Dr. Stearns saying, "Humphrey is a splendid fellow and very popular with everyone—he will do good work if placed with a boy who will not take his attention from the regular study periods. . . . May I ask that you take a personal interest in the boy so that he will get started on the right path which will, I am sure, lead to a successful year."

From the very beginning Humphrey disliked the academy. There was no one at the train at Andover to greet him. He found that he was expected to be on his own and it took him a long time to find a wagon to haul his trunks to Taylor Hall, one of the newer dormitories, where he had been assigned a room on the second floor.

His room, No. 5, boasted a fireplace and was furnished with a steel cot, a small oak desk, a bureau, an oak armchair, and a sizable closet. Happily, the single bathroom that serviced the other six occupants on the floor was next to his room.

Frederick M. Boyce, a physics teacher and the housemaster, lived on the ground floor with his wife and children. From the beginning "Freddie" made it plain that he would brook no shenanigans. But he seriously warned that there would be little time for anything other than study anyway.

The other boys on the floor were cordial but, to Humphrey's mind, bookworms. Charles Yardley Chittick, now a patent attorney in Boston, had the room across the hall. "If there's anything I remember about Humphrey in those days, it was his sullenness," Mr. Chittick says. "I got the impression that he was a very spoiled boy. When things didn't go his way he didn't like it a bit."

By Christmas vacation Humphrey was in drastic difficulties at Andover, failing three of his five courses. When he went home for Christmas vacation he tried to avoid showing Dr. Bogart his report card, but it was his mother who was most upset. Dr. Bogart explained optimistically that it would take time for the boy to get adjusted, but she was insistent that his grades improve at once. "If your marks don't improve measurably by the end of the next semester, we will withdraw you and put you to work," Mrs. Bogart threatened. On that note Humphrey returned to school.

The following month, February 19, 1918, Dr. Stearns wrote Dr. Bogart that the faculty voted to put Humphrey on probation because "of the poor record which he has made this term . . . all of his teachers agree that he has good ability but that he has not exerted himself at all seriously during the current term; and that his low standing at the present time is due largely to that fact. It was also decided that his work in English should be readjusted, as he seems wholly unable at this time to meet the requirements of that particular course."

Dr. Stearns concluded with the warning that "if there is not an all-around improvement we shall be compelled to require his withdrawal. I earnestly hope that such a catastrophe as this may be avoided."

Dr. Bogart instantly replied, saying that he and Mrs. Bogart would do everything in their power "to have the boy find himself. Humphrey is a good boy, with no bad habits, who simply has lost his head temporarily," he wrote. "The whole problem to my mind seems to be that the boy has given up his mind to sports and continuous correspondence with his girl friends. . . . The harder the screws are put on the better it will be for my son."

Apparently Humphrey did not respond well to the "screws." On May 15, 1918, Dr. Stearns wrote: "To my great regret I am forced to advise you that Humphrey has failed to meet the terms of his probation and that it becomes necessary therefore for us to require his withdrawal from the school at this time. I was not present at the faculty meeting when this decision was reached; but I have learned from the boy's instructors that it was the unanimous opinion of those who are familiar with the situation that it would be unwise for Humphrey to remain here longer. I cannot tell you how deeply I regret our inability to make the boy realize the seriousness of the situation and put forth the effort required to avert this disaster.

"My experience, covering a good many years now, leads me to believe that Humphrey will profit greatly by this seemingly unfortunate occurrence, and that it will tend to bring him to his senses as nothing else could do. I can only express the sincere hope that this will prove the turning point in the boy's life, and that from now on he will develop that serious purpose which he appears to have lacked thus far. . . ."

Two days later, in Dr. Bogart's absence "on business," Maude Humphrey answered Dr. Stearns. "I am sending Humphrey $25.00 to come home at once," she wrote, adding, "Mr. Frank E. Kirby, a very prominent naval architect, and now building ships for the government, has promised to give Humphrey a job in his shipyard at once. I trust the boy will come to his senses and work. As Mr. Kirby has both brains and influence (he bought all the ships for

the U.S. government the time of the Spanish-American War)
I hope he can help Humphrey. . . ."

Years later Bogart claimed that he was asked to leave Andover because of his "excessive high spirits" and "infrac-
tions of the rules." At various times he said he ducked an
assistant professor in a fountain or, alternately, that he
sneaked out at night to watch a fire and was spotted by a
young teacher, a track man, who gave chase and caught him.

Mr. Chittick, who remembers the fire and accompanied
Humphrey to see it, said the entire escapade was without
incident. He also said he never heard of Humphrey's duck-
ing an assistant professor in a fountain, an episode that
would certainly have been discussed at the school if it had
happened.

Humphrey's report card does not indicate any disciplinary
difficulties. It does show, however, that he was not a good student. He failed five of his seven subjects—Bible, chemistry,
English, French, and solid geometry—and he received a D
in algebra.

"The problem was the way I was taught," he explained
later. "They made you learn dates and that was all. They'd
say, 'A war was fought in 1812.' So what? They never told
you why people decided to kill each other at just that
moment.

"And I hated the smugness of people in authority. I can't
show reverence when I don't feel it. I was always testing my
instructors to see if they were as bright or godlike as they
seemed to be."

Humphrey's homecoming was stormy. His father was
quietly but deeply disappointed. It was apparent that Humphrey could never go on to Yale.

Mrs. Bogart was harsh. "You've had every chance that
could be given to you and you have failed—not only yourself but your parents," she said. "We don't intend to support
you for the rest of your life. You're on your own from now
on."

Humphrey moped about the house for several weeks. Then,
when he learned that a friend, Stuart Rose, had joined the
army and gone to the Mexican border, he decided to enlist
in the navy. Although he was barely of age, he had his
parents' consent and the blessings of Dr. Stearns, who in
July, 1918, wrote, "I am delighted to hear that Humphrey
has entered active service. . . . The boy is all right at heart
and is bound to come out on top in the end. Increased re-

sponsibilities are frequently the making of a boy of Humphrey's tendencies. . . ."

Humphrey had more practical grounds for enlisting: It would enable him to get away from home and the sarcastic needling of his mother about what a ne'er-do-well he was.

"The war was a big joke," he said years later. "Death? What does death mean to a kid of eighteen? The idea of death starts getting to you only when you're older—when you read obituaries of famous people whose accomplishments have touched you, and when people of your own generation die. At eighteen war was great stuff. Paris! French girls! Hot damn!"

At training camp Humphrey was a messenger, one of whose jobs was to carry the list of those assigned to overseas duty from HQ to the Embarkation Officer. Realizing he was a long way from those French girls, he would have us believe he boldly typed his own name on the bottom of the list. Though this bravado seems unlikely, he eventually was assigned to convoy duty aboard a troop transport—the *Leviathan*, formerly the *Vaterland*, Germany's largest passenger liner, which had been converted to a U.S. troop carrier.

He saw action the second day out, though not from the Germans. A husky young officer ordered him to do something, and Seaman Bogart, challenger of authority, replied, "That's not my detail."

The next moment he was sprawled on the deck, holding an aching jaw. He got to his feet—and at attention. "Don't say that again when you're given an order," the officer said. It was Seaman Bogart's first encounter with the kind of discipline he understood. He did not repeat the offense.

He spent all of the next year aboard the *Leviathan*, shuttling troops back and forth between Hoboken, Brest, and Liverpool. The skipper of the *Leviathan*, Captain J. S. Oman, was a tough character. When, through a mistake in orders, Humphrey took a shore leave just at the time he was supposed to be returning from one, he was posted as a deserter. At Captain's Mast, when the Old Man gave him ten days in the brig, Humphrey answered back. Within seconds he was given twenty, then thirty days.

Ruth Rankin, a girl who dated him at that time, says she never saw a sailor "who did more for the uniform, whenever he happened to be out of the brig." A contem-

porary photograph shows Humphrey as a petulantly handsome young man with a big grin.

Most of the time Seaman Bogart stayed just short of the
brig, but he was confined to the ship often enough so that
he missed many of his shore leaves. One of his most unhappy war memories, he recalled later, came after a cross-
ing in which he had avoided all trouble: He lost a month's
pay in a crap game the night before the ship reached port
in France.

All told, Humphrey made between fifteen and twenty
crossings aboard the *Leviathan*. On one occasion the ship
was shelled by a U-boat. A splinter of wood from a burst
pierced his upper lip. Although the ship's doctor did a neat
job of patching the wound up, a nerve was damaged and
the lip was left partly paralyzed. Humphrey's mouth from
then on had that tight-set look that was to become a domi-
nant feature of his appearance. The wound also affected his
speech—he talked with a slight lisp.

Soon after that incident, on the morning of November
11, 1918, President Wilson announced that the Armistice had
been signed. Dr. James Mitchell, now chief physician for
MGM studios in Hollywood, was then a chief pharmacist's
mate in the navy and a friend of Humphrey's. He recalls
that the captain told Humphrey, a chief yeoman, to make
out discharges for 200 of the most deserving men.

"Humphrey went below and made out his own discharge
first," Dr. Mitchell said. "He was about to go over the side
with seabag and hammock in hand when the captain spied
him and asked where he was going. Humphrey answered that
he had orders to discharge the most deserving men first, and
he thought he was the most deserving man aboard ship. The
captain insisted he go below and finish out his service time."

Humphrey was almost twenty years old and had been in
the navy for two years when he was finally given an honor-
able discharge. Later, he said he was "sorry that the war
had not touched me mentally. I was still no nearer to an
understanding of what I wanted to be or what I was."

Humphrey went back to his third-floor room in the family
brownstone at 103rd Street. Although the Armistice had
been signed, there was no peace at home. His mother constantly belittled him, pointing out what he knew all too well
himself—he had little education and no way of earning a
living.

Dr. Bogart was more sympathetic—when he was around.

The doctor had taken to signing on as ship's doctor on freighters and Humphrey claimed that his father had become a morphine addict. For this there is no corroborative evidence, although addiction is not infrequent among doctors. In any event, Humphrey listened alone to his mother's constant complaint about the men of the house, who were good for nothing, willing to let her support the family.

During the next two years Humphrey made an indifferent attempt to join the business world. An old Warner Brothers biography that called for him to list jobs he had held indicates that he worked after his navy discharge as an inspector of tugs for the Pennsylvania Railroad for $30 a week.

In a story, probably apocryphal since there is no other record of his working for the railroad, Humphrey said that one day his supervisor took him aside to say if he worked hard he might one day have a chance to be president of the railroad. "When I found that there were 50,000 employees between me and the president, I quit," the biography quotes him as saying.

It is a matter of record, however, that he worked for at least a year as a runner for the Wall Street investment house of S. W. Strauss & Co. Presumably it was no coincidence that the firm handled his parents' investments—it appears that the Bogarts had not yet given up trying to help their son.

Those were the opening days of the Roaring Twenties. Miss Humphrey and the other suffragettes had secured the right to vote and were abandoning the last vestiges of Victorianism in dress, speech, and thought. Women were discussing Freud over cigarettes (in long holders, to be sure), drinking cocktails, bobbing their hair, and wearing lipstick and rouge. A *New York Times* editorial lamented, "The American woman has lifted her skirts beyond any modest limitation."

The Eighteenth Amendment brought Prohibition, and with it the Jazz Age complete with speakeasies, bathtub gin, bootleggers, and gangsters machine-gunning one another down in broad daylight, just as in the movies Bogart was to make years later.

Miss Rankin, who dated Humphrey frequently in those days, recalls that they "virtually thrived" on the masquerade brawls in Webster Hall and the Kit Kat Club. "We did Greenwich Village regularly, which we considered to be slumming."

Villagers tended then, as they do now, to resent this attitude of uptowners. Mrs. Lee Gershwin, wife of Ira Gershwin, the famous librettist, was living on West 8th Street in the Village when she first met Humphrey.

"Although he was an attractive boy, Humphrey wasn't very popular with our crowd," she recalls. "For one thing, he ate onions, and he didn't write poetry. In fact, he didn't do anything interesting that I can recall."

Years later when Bogart and Miss Rankin were recalling those early days their dialogue gave an indication of the kind of life he was leading.

Bogart: "Do you remember the time your Stutz ran out of gas on the Queensborough Bridge at three A.M. and I had to push it over the rise so we could coast off?"

Miss Rankin: "Remember the time we ran into the elevated post on Sixth Avenue? And what the cop said? And the time we went to court with a speeding ticket, and the cop lied like a gentleman—said we were doing only forty—so we took him to lunch at Rector's. He ordered everything in the place, and we had only two dollars between us, so he had to pay the check? Did you ever look him up and pay it back?"

Bogart: "Madame, you will never find a Bogart lacking in the finer principles. Besides, what if he had caught me speeding after that?"

Miss Rankin: "He couldn't, because your father wouldn't let you have the car. You always smashed it."

Bogart: "The last time it was your fault. Remember that masquerade at Webster Hall—you wore two beads and a buckle, and I was a Spanish toreador—very hot stuff? And the fenders were off the Stutz to have the wrinkles ironed out and the headlights wouldn't work, so we drove past the new subway excavation and picked up red lanterns and tied them all over the car. And then it began to rain pitchforks, so we arrived at the party soaked and covered with mud. Were we sights!

"So we retired to the ladies' and gents' room to take a bath, with thousands of people milling around. And you were the belle of the ball because most of your beads dissolved."

It was all very much Jazz Age stuff, but Humphrey, brought up in propriety and the Horatio Alger tradition, felt guilty because he was not working at a job with a future. He constantly groused about being an errand boy to his friends, Bill Brady and Bill's older half sister, Alice.

One night Alice suggested that Humphrey see her father about a job. Bill, Sr., was starting an independent movie company, World Films. He was about to make a picture starring Nita Naldi and Arlene Pretty. Humphrey took the advice and was hired as an office boy, with the promise that Mr. Brady would "give him a chance."

Toward the end of a picture called *Life*, with Arlene Pretty and Rod LaRocque, Brady discharged the director and told Humphrey that this was his chance: He was to finish directing the picture. Bogart tried, but was so inept that Brady had to take charge himself.

Although Humphrey couldn't direct *Life*, he felt he could write a better story. He began drifting into Greenwich Village every afternoon, where he tried at least to look like a writer, sitting in Chumley's, surrounded by book jackets contributed by the successful clientele. After a few months he submitted a story to Mr. Brady. Brady said it had an interesting plot and passed it on to Jesse L. Lasky. He, in turn, gave it to his assistant, Walter Wanger, who referred the story to the wastebasket. "It was awful," Mr. Wanger recalled, although he was later fond of saying, "Bogart once wrote for me."

At Alice Brady's suggestion, Mr. Brady made Humphrey stage manager of one of his plays at $50 a week. Then the producer's wife, actress Grace George, suggested Humphrey stage-manage her new play, *The Ruined Lady*.

During the run of the play, Neil Hamilton, who was the juvenile lead, became ill. Brady required that the stage manager understudy all the male roles, so Humphrey read Hamilton's lines to Miss George. A rehearsal was called, and on a Saturday afternoon Humphrey Bogart made his first professional appearance, with just the cast as audience.

"It was awful," Bogart said years later. "I knew all the lines of all the parts because I'd heard them from out front about a thousand times. But I took one look at the emptiness where the audience would be that night and I couldn't remember anything."

Fortunately, Miss George also became ill before curtain time, so the play closed that night. Humphrey's debut was postponed.

Working for Brady was always exciting, Bogart has said. One could never tell what the producer might do next. Often

he would step in two days before an opening and tear the
play to pieces. The actors would have to stay up all night
putting the pieces back together.

One memorable night in Atlantic City, Brady kicked Humphrey in the stomach. It was the opening of a play called
Drifting, starring Alice Brady. Mr. Brady hated long inter-
missions and sometimes arbitrarily shortened them by ringing the curtain back up himself. This particular night Brady
brought the curtain up early enough to give the audience a
good view of stagehands moving scenery. Bogart rang it
down again. Brady flushed with anger and gave his stage
manager a good one in the midsection with his foot.

Humphrey bided his time. Later that evening, when the
curtain was down and Mr. Brady was on stage making last-
minute preparations for the next act, Bogart sent the curtain
up. The set was a bar in Manchuria with only one white
man, the bartender, in the scene. The rest were wild Man-
churian natives—plus Mr. Brady, looking decidedly out of
place. Brady was bewildered for a moment, then remembered he had once been an actor. In a loud voice he asked
for cigarettes. The bartender handed them to him. Brady
threw a coin on the bar, stalked offstage, and promptly fired
Bogart. Humphrey, who had been fired and rehired with
some regularity, gleefully departed, but was accepted back
on the job the next day.

Later, when the play opened at the Fulton Theater in
Brooklyn, Brady, who had overheard Humphrey needling
some of the actors about their easy jobs, said he was going to
make an actor of him. He gave Bogart one line of dialogue
as a Japanese houseboy.

The first time Humphrey trod the boards, Stuart Rose was
in the audience with Humphrey's sister Pat (Frances), whom
Rose was courting, and Dr. Bogart.

"Humphrey came onstage carrying a tray of cocktails. He
said his one line and he embarrassed me it was so bad," recalls Mr. Rose. "But Dr. Bogart turned to me, put a hand on
my knee, and said, 'The boy is good, isn't he?' Of course I
said, 'Yes, he is.' "

Humphrey must have impressed Brady too, because his
next part was as the juvenile in *Swifty,* starring Frances
Howard (now Mrs. Sam Goldwyn) and Neil Hamilton. His
role this time was seventy sides long.

Brady taught the young actor a good deal. He gave what
he called "What?" rehearsals, in which he would sit in the

back of the balcony listening to the actors onstage. When someone was inaudible in his lines he would roar, "What?" Bogart, slightly handicapped by his lisp, soon learned not to mumble.

There was one scene in which Humphrey had to rush downstairs with a gun and shout at Hamilton, "I'll kill you, I'll kill you, I'll kill you!" Mr. Brady sat in the pit watching the scene and making Bogart do it over and over again. Finally, as a devastating comment on Bogart's acting, he fell asleep—or pretended to.

Humphrey, furious, shoved Hamilton aside and went charging after Mr. Brady, who came roaring right back at him. Bill, Jr., and Hamilton caught Bogart and took him into the alley until he cooled off.

On opening night Humphrey was so nervous that he had to walk offstage to get a glass of water, leaving Hamilton to ad-lib. Brady was upset. So were the critics.

Bogart later recalled how his mother woke him up the morning after his acting debut by bringing the papers to his bedroom. Sitting on the edge of his bed, she rattled the papers before him. "I will read you the reviews," she said grimly. She chose Alexander Woollcott's notice first. " 'The young man who embodies the aforesaid sprig'—that's you, my boy—'was what might mercifully be described as inadequate.' "

Swifty closed very shortly after it opened, but it did impress one person. She was Rosalie Stewart, the producer, who called Humphrey to say she had seen something in him. She offered him a part as a newspaperman in *Meet the Wife,* with Mary Boland and Clifton Webb, and the show played at the Klaw Theater for thirty weeks.

The popularity of the theater is indicated by fifty-one productions playing in New York at that time. The phenomenon of the day was *Abie's Irish Rose,* because of its survival despite the savage assaults of the critics. But theatergoers also had a choice of Jeanne Eagels in *Rain,* Walter Hampden in *Cyrano de Bergerac, Charlot's Revue,* which introduced Gertrude Lawrence and Beatrice Lillie to New York, or *White Cargo,* which ran for 900 performances.

Humphrey was finally in a hit show and, it seemed, in the big time. Even his mother was impressed, though she never became convinced that actors were socially acceptable. Dr. Bogart, however, was genuinely pleased that his son had found something for which he seemed to be fitted.

With Bill Brady, Jr., Humphrey began to enjoy his increased income and to take an active part in the Roaring Twenties. It was still the Prohibition Era, and nothing could be more romantic—or flattering—than to stand in front of the peephole of a barred door and, on recognition, gain admittance to the forbidden revelry and boozing going on inside.

They saw Texas Guinan in her own club, and when it was padlocked by Prohibition agents they followed her to her new club, the El Fey. They cheered the opening of Clayton, Jackson & Durante at the Dover Club, and with the rest of the speakeasy crowd enjoyed the *Variety* report that Eddie Jackson had refused a $1,000 bill as salary payment, because no big salary should be paid in such a small way. "He wanted all fives—in a bundle," *Variety* explained.

For a change of scenery they drove uptown to Harlem's Next, Small's Paradise, Connie's Inn, or the Cotton Club, which was the cream of the so-called "mob joints" in Harlem. A routine evening's entertainment for Humphrey and his friends was dinner after the show at a conservative hotel, restaurant, or speakeasy. That was followed by a tour of the night spots, ending at dawn in some hot and low-down saloon. Then to bed—if one was fortunate, and Bogart usually was—in some warmhearted lady's hideaway provided by a rich butter-and-egg man.

Show-business people, even more than most, were caught up in the twenties' frenetic search for excitement. Although Humphrey never missed a performance, it was not uncommon for him to come to work after not having had any sleep at all the preceding twenty-four hours.

One night, a week before *Meet the Wife* was to close, Humphrey stayed too long at a party. At that evening's performance he blew his lines, causing Miss Boland to ad-lib frantically for minutes while he leaned sweating against a wall, his eyes glazed. As the descending curtain's shadow reached his chin, Miss Boland turned on him in fury and announced, "Get this, Bogart—you'll never work in another play with me!"

But Humphrey kept working, alternating between actor and stage manager. Photographs taken at the time show how handsome he was. He most often played romantic juveniles in what he called "Tennis, anyone?" parts.

"The playwright gets five or six characters into a scene and doesn't know how to get them offstage," he once explained.

"So what does he do? He drags in the juvenile, who has been waiting in the wings for just such a chance. He comes in, tennis racquet under his arm, and says, 'How about a game of tennis?'

"That, of course, solves the playwright's problem. The players whom the author wants to get rid of for the time being accept the suggestion. The leading lady, who is due for a love scene with the leading man, declines. So the others exit and all is ready for the love game between the leading lady and man.

"It doesn't always have to be tennis—sometimes it's golf or riding—but tennis is better because it gives the young man a chance to look attractive in spotless white flannels."

Early in 1924, Humphrey opened in *Nerves*, starring Kenneth MacKenna, Paul Kelly, and a lovely actress, Mary Philips. A war play, *Nerves* had the misfortune to be running opposite *What Price Glory?* It ran only a few weeks, but Bogart got favorable reviews from the critics.

"The notices gave me a badly swelled head," Bogart once said. "In one scene, while I was delivering a very dramatic speech, Mary Philips was supposed to walk away from me saying nothing. One night I noticed that she was putting a lot of *that* into her walk—so much so that the audience focused their attention on her instead of me," he said. "After the show I bawled her out plenty for stealing my scene. 'You can't do that,' I told her. 'That's my scene.' There was an amused twinkle in her eyes as she looked at me. 'Suppose you try to stop me,' she challenged. Well, I didn't try to stop her, because while I was talking I suddenly became aware that here was a girl with whom I could very easily fall in love."

After the play closed, Bogart forgot about Mary Philips. He went back to work for Brady again as stage manager of a touring company of *Drifting*. A short time after the opening Alice Brady, who was the star despite her well-advanced pregnancy, came unseasonably to her time on a Saturday night. By Monday morning another actress had to be found and coached to replace her. All day Sunday a frantic assistant stage manager ran through the lines with one Minna Gombell downstairs, while in an unused upstairs office Humphrey cued a talented redhead named Helen Menken.

Miss Menken got the part. On her opening night Bogart, who had a complicated stage with eight sets to manage, had problems. Most of the sets fell down, some on Miss Menken.

A fiercely articulate young woman who had been onstage since she was six, she turned loose a spate of fiery temper on Bogart. Later he said, "I guess I shouldn't have done it, but I booted her. She, in turn, belted me and ran to her dressing room to cry."

On that promising note he commenced to court Miss Menken, who, though older than he and far more successful, seemed flattered by his attentions. Within a few weeks they decided they were in love and took out a marriage license. But Humphrey was wary of the responsibility of supporting a wife. His career in the theater seemed too uncertain. The license wasn't used.

Then he went into Herman Gantvoort's production of *Hell's Bells,* with Shirley Booth. It played at Wallack's Theater for fifteen weeks, and then Humphrey was out of work again. Luckily, Mary Boland had forgotten her pique and asked him to be in her new show, a comedy entitled *Cradle Snatchers,* with Edna May Oliver and Raymond Hackett.

His reviews were good. Amy Leslie, one of Chicago's leading critics, wrote: ". . . he is as young and handsome as Valentino and elegant in comedy as E. H. Sothern, as graceful as any of our best actors."

His growing reputation, plus Miss Menken's encouragement, persuaded Humphrey to give up stage managing and devote himself full time to an acting career—even though he seemed doomed to remain a juvenile.

He continued to drink more than he could comfortably hold, in the fashion of the times. One of his favorite haunts was Tony's on 52nd Street. Tony's was superficially indistinguishable from any ordinary speakeasy—a cellar entrance, a bar, a kitchen. Nothing was plush, nothing glittered, except the patrons. Tony's was a special hangout of writers and actors, and any night of the week the barflies might include Heywood Broun, Alexander Woollcott, Howard and Betty Dietz, Dorothy Parker, and Mark Hellinger. They went there because they could drink and talk with their own kind, and because Tony Soma, the proprietor, loved actors and writers. He would carry a favorite's bar bill for years and never mention it.

Tony was a student of Yoga and used to urge his customers to try the exercises. Humphrey was one of the few who would go along with Tony, perhaps because it increased his credit. He was constantly kidded by the other patrons, however, "for accepting his weekly salary under false pretenses," for daring to call himself an actor. Producer Leonard Sillman recalls Humphrey standing at the bar, taking a ribbing from the sharp-tongued crowd until he got pitifully tanked, then going into the kitchen to stand on his head.

"The needling I got about my acting in those days just made me mad," Bogart once said. "It made me want to keep on until I'd get to the point where I didn't stink any more."

Helen Menken had gone on from *Drifting* to become the toast of Broadway in Austin Strong's *Seventh Heaven*. Humphrey's show, *Cradle Snatchers,* was also a hit, and although her income was larger by far than his and her prospects were brighter, she still wanted to get married. Miss Menken was convinced that through her friendship with Alec Woollcott, the most powerful critic of the day, she could help Humphrey's career.

Humphrey discussed the situation with young Bill Brady and Stuart Rose over a bottle of beer at Tony's. He added up the pluses and the minuses. Primarily, his reluctance to marry Helen was based on the fact that she was more successful than he, and he was afraid that she might try to wear the pants in the family. He had seen enough of that in his own home.

The friends listened sympathetically, agreeing that Helen was a strong woman who might also put career before marriage someday.

"But," Bill Brady warned, "you're in too deep now. If you don't marry her, you'll never get on the Broadway stage again. Alec will tar and feather you."

The marriage license they had taken out some four years earlier was still valid. On May 20, 1926, they were married at the Gramercy Park Hotel in New York City, with Stuart Rose as best man. Both bride and groom signed the marriage register as being twenty-six years old.

The parents of the bride were deaf-mutes, and the Reverend John Kent, who performed the service, was deaf. Mr. Rose recalls the wedding ceremony as "a macabre performance. The deaf minister had learned to talk and he insisted on reading the service in a kind of horrible singsong while at the same time he spelled it in sign language. After the ceremony, Helen had hysterics and refused to see the reporters gathered in the lobby. The whole thing was just too much for her."

The marriage, which commenced on such a sour note, got

worse instead of better. "We quarreled over the most inconsequential things, such as whether it would be right to feed the dog caviar when people were starving," Bogart said. "I contended that the dog should eat hamburger and like it. She held out for caviar. What started out to be just a little difference of opinion would suddenly become a battle royal, with one or the other of us walking out in a fine rage."

They had been married only a few months when *Cradle Snatchers* closed after running forty-two weeks, the longest run of the 1925–26 season. Early in January, 1927, Roscoe "Fatty" Arbuckle, who had been trying to fight his way back to popularity after a lurid Hollywood scandal involving a girl's death, made his reappearance on Broadway as featured comedian in *Baby Mine*. Humphrey had a featured role in the production. Although Mr. Arbuckle's reception was friendly as far as the public was concerned, the play could not sustain him nor he the play. After two weeks both were off Broadway, along with Humphrey, who jumped right into the cast of *Saturday's Children* when Roger Pryor was taken ill in the middle of the Chicago run.

Humphrey demanded that Helen accompany him to Chicago, but she wanted to try out for a new play. They separated, and although they tried to patch things up several times, they never succeeded. After one disastrous attempt at Edgewater Beach, when she claimed he blackened her eyes, she went to London to play in the English company of *Seventh Heaven*.

After a year and a half of marriage, during which they lived together only a few months, Miss Menken filed for divorce. According to a story in the old *New York Herald* she charged: "I tried to make my marriage the paramount interest of my life. Although my career was a success, I was willing to give it up and concentrate my interests on a home. I was deeply interested in acting, but I felt that the managing of a home was something greater. I had planned to make a home for my husband, but he did not want a home. He regarded his career as of far more importance than married life."

Humphrey, then on Broadway in *Saturday's Children*, did not comment on the suit. Miss Menken waived alimony. Years later she told Lauren Bacall, "I was to blame for the breakup of our marriage. I put my career first and my marriage second."

Humphrey was then twenty-seven years old. His improving talent and the vaguely Valentinoesque cast of his features had helped establish him as a juvenile. But he was not going to remain suitable for such roles much longer. Like most aging juveniles he lived from day to day in the hope of a break—a role that would establish him as either a leading man or a heavy.

When he was not working, his life was one extended hangover. With Bill Brady, Jr., he was a familiar figure at dozens of speakeasies now almost forgotten—the Dizzy Club, the Hotsy Totsy, Chez Florence, Basque's, the Aquarium, Mario's, the Clamhouse, the Bandbox—all running wide open as Prohibition became more and more a joke.

It might be unfair to say that he and Brady supported those clubs, but they had running tabs at most and certainly could be considered major contributors. And always there were pretty girls around. Bogart never discussed his conquests, but years later he did admit to a friend in Hollywood that he and young Bill cut quite a swath among the Broadway chorus girls. "I had had enough women by the time I was twenty-seven to know what I was looking for in a wife the next time I married," he said.

What he claimed he wanted was "a girl I could come home to, a Roaming in the Gloaming type." Nevertheless he persisted in forming attachments with actresses—ladies who are not noted for lingering by the hearth.

One night, after seeing the first talkie, Al Jolson in *The Jazz Singer*, Humphrey went backstage at a nearby theater to visit actress Mary Halliday. Another actress in the dressing room looked familiar. It was Mary Philips, the girl he once thought he could be in love with.

She was small and his type. She also remembered him—apparently not unfavorably. When he invited her to a drink at Sardi's she accepted. Soon, with Mary as a substitute for Bill Brady, Humphrey continued his endless tour of the speakeasies, conducting a courtship between drinks.

Although Mary was not a beauty in the flashy vogue of the day, she was attractive, encouraging, and understanding. She believed, as he did, that actors belonged on Broadway, not in Hollywood. And she encouraged him to learn more about his profession. Their circle of friends was all show-business people. When Humphrey wasn't working he was seeing plays or talking about acting.

One summer Sunday he and Mary went to spend the

afternoon in the country with Holbrook Blinn, who was then an established star., She remembers that Humphrey asked Blinn how he could get a reputation as an actor.

"Just keep working," Blinn said. "If you're always busy, somebody is going to get the idea that you must be good."

Humphrey pondered the advice for a moment. Then he asked another question, "Holbrook, you're not any taller than I am, but you appear tall on the stage. How do you manage that?"

Blinn stood up and took a few steps, his back to Humphrey. Then he turned around and before everyone's eyes he seemed to grow in stature.

"Just think tall," he said.

Miss Philips recalls Humphrey in those days as a "strangely puritanical man with very old-fashioned virtues. He had class as well as charm."

Humphrey had competition for Mary from Kenneth MacKenna, a handsome young leading man and his friend as well as hers. Kenneth proposed first, but Mary waited to see if Humphrey was going to propose too. Despite Kenneth's pleas that she consider longer before making up her mind, Mary quickly accepted Humphrey.

Almost a year to the day after he had been divorced from Helen Menken, Humphrey and Mary Philips were married at her mother's home in Hartford, Connecticut, after a matinee performance of *Saturday's Children*. He was twenty-eight. She was twenty-five.

"Mary is a mixture of New England and Irish, and she furnishes just the sort of balance wheel I need," Humphrey told a reporter on their wedding day. "Marrying her is probably the most wonderful thing that could happen to me."

Their marriage seemed to get off to a good start. They were both working steadily. When *Saturday's Children* closed, he went right into *Skyrocket*, which failed miserably, but again Alice Brady came to the rescue. Miss Brady, who had become one of the highest-paid stars on Broadway, asked for Humphrey to play a featured role in her current play, *A Most Immoral Lady*. It ran for 160 performances.

Later in 1929, when David Belasco went into rehearsal with *It's a Wise Child*, he gave Humphrey a role along with Mildred McCoy, Minor Watson, and Sidney Toler. When the comedy opened it was the sensation of the season.

Life was a wonderful merry-go-round for the newlyweds,

with the brass ring always within reach. But in October of 1929 the gay music had some sour notes. *The New York Times* reported to panic-stricken readers: "The second hurricane of liquidation within four days hit the stock market yesterday. It came suddenly, and violently. . . ."

The crash hit the films, already rocked by the advent of sound, particularly hard. Business slumped so badly that one theater offered two-for-one tickets and coupons entitling patrons to free Marcel waves. Hollywood desperately needed leading men who could both act and talk. They frantically searched the ranks of Broadway players while trying to teach stars of the silent films how to talk.

Stuart Rose, who had married Humphrey's sister Frances, was story editor of Fox Films and the right-hand man of Al Lewis, head of the New York office. The studio owned that hardy perennial, *The Man Who Came Back*. Originally they had planned to cast their silent stars Janet Gaynor and Charles Farrell in it but decided instead to use new actors in the hope of making new stars.

They tested almost every actor on Broadway, but the results were dismal. Stuart suggested that his boss test Humphrey, but Mr. Lewis, echoing the Broadway opinion, snorted, "He wears a white tie and tails well, but all he can say is 'Anyone for tennis?' "

"He can act," persisted Stuart. "He can play anything." Humphrey, who was still in *It's a Wise Child*, finally was given a chance. "A very, very fine test," recalls Mr. Rose.

With a contract and train tickets for Los Angeles in his pocket, Humphrey rushed home to ask Mary to quit her play and come with him. It was the first time that he would be able to support her completely, and he was full of plans for going out to the Coast in style and living there in the grand manner. A $500-a-week actor when he worked on Broadway, his film contract called for him to be paid $750 a week, more than he had ever dreamed he would be earning.

Mary refused to leave her play. She had a contract and, she said, her career was in New York. Since they were a "modern couple," though, they agreed that he was to date other girls while he was away, and she could go out with whom she liked.

On that somewhat chilly note Humphrey left for Los Angeles, after sending a telegram announcing his impending arrival to two actor friends, Bobby Ames and Mary's ex-suitor, Kenneth MacKenna.

When he arrived at the Los Angeles station Humphrey got a big greeting from his friends, who then asked why he had come west.

"I've come to play the lead in *The Man Who Came Back*," Humphrey said.

The two greeters doubled up with laughter. Each of them had been brought to Hollywood for the same part, which eventually was given to Charles Farrell. It was Humphrey, however, who was assigned as Farrell's voice coach.

Six weeks later, Humphrey wrote a plaintive letter to Stuart Rose asking, "What in the hell am I doing here being paid $750.00 a week to coach a very nice fellow named Charles Farrell to play a role he can't play because he can't talk?"

After finishing with Farrell, Humphrey was given a role in *A Devil with Women* starring Victor McLaglen. He played a rich youngster, a "Tennis, anyone?" juvenile again.

His next film was a John Ford comedy starring Spencer Tracy, who had recently come out from the Broadway stage and had started to make it big in Hollywood. While working with him on that film, Humphrey began his lifelong friendship with Tracy.

In his third picture, *Body and Soul*, Humphrey played with Charles Farrell, the man he had been brought to Hollywood to coach. Farrell was still resentful of the young Broadway actor. When director Alfred Santell asked Humphrey to give Farrell more tips on talking, the silent star's resentment turned into open hostility.

The picture was about World War I aviators, and Humphrey and Farrell had two weeks of night work, during which they were packed into the cockpit of a plane. Their bickering was constant. "Move over" and "Keep on your side" worked up to "If you think I'm going to take that off you . . ."

When the last scene was finished, Humphrey angrily extended an invitation to Farrell to take a walk in the alley.

Outside, Farrell calmly asked, "Can you fight?"

"What do you mean, can I fight? I can lick you," Humphrey said.

"Yeah, but can you fight?" Farrell persisted. "It's only fair to tell you I was boxing champion in college, and I know how to fight."

That stopped Humphrey. He decided to talk it over. They ended up by agreeing to go on a vacation on Farrell's boat. Ultimately they became good friends.

Most of the other pictures Humphrey made during the

sixteen months he remained in Hollywood are notable not
because of their excellence but because of the other players
in them.

He had a small part in *Bad Sister,* in which Bette Davis
made her film debut. He played a bit role in *Women of All
Nations*, starring Victor McLaglen. Then he was signed for
Holy Terror, a Western starring George O'Brien. "I was too
short to be a cowboy," he later recalled, "so they gave me
elevator shoes and padded out my shoulders. I walked around
as though I was on stilts and felt like a dummy."

Next was *Love Affair*, with Dorothy Mackaill, followed by
Big City Blues. In that picture, directed by Mervyn LeRoy,
Humphrey got tenth billing. The star was Joan Blondell. He
played a gangster for the first time in another LeRoy film,
Three on a Match, starring Miss Blondell and, again, Bette
Davis.

With the remarkable prescience that frequently character-
izes film producers, someone decided there was no future for
Humphrey in movies. The decision was made on the basis of
his scarred lip and slight lisp. Women would never go for
him, the executive said, so Humphrey's contract was dropped.

His homecoming was less than triumphant. Mary confessed
she had fallen in love with Roland Young, whom she had met
on tour. Humphrey, more hurt than he would admit, turned
to Bill Brady for advice. "You both left yourselves open to
this sort of thing with your 'arrangement.' " Bill said. "Would
it have been better if you had been the one to fall in love
with someone else? And if you had, what would you expect
Mary to do?"

Humphrey pondered the question a moment. He admitted
he hadn't been entirely blameless. Over such a long period as
his stay in Hollywood, it was scarcely surprising that something of the sort had happened. Since Mary had been honest
with him and readily promised not to see the man again, he
would have to swallow his ego. But he did learn a lesson—
never be separated from his wife again, if he wanted to stay
married.

With some difficulty he and Mary resumed their marriage.
He began doing the rounds, looking for work again, surprised
to find that no one on Broadway was impressed that he had
been making films in Hollywood. In fact, most producers
weren't even aware that he had been away.

He rehearsed a total of twenty weeks for four plays, none
of which ran more than a week. On a deal that guaranteed

him a percentage of the profits he appeared in *Our Wife*, which opened on March 4, 1933, the day President Roosevelt declared a Bank Holiday. There were ten people in the opening night audience. Humphrey earned just $56.00 in the first week of the show, which closed after twenty performances.

He had a short run at the Guild Theater in a comedy, *The Mask and the Face*, followed by a part in an All-Star Universal film made in New York entitled *Midnight*. Again he played a gangster. Again, his performance passed unnoticed.

Although jobs were few and brief, so that he was unable to support himself and Mary, he did get some satisfaction from the fact that he was gradually perfecting his craft.

"There's an awful lot of bunk written about acting," he said years later. "But it isn't easy. You can't just make faces. If you make yourself feel the way the character would feel, your face will express the right things—if you're an actor. There are lots of things to learn. Try walking up to a door and opening it some time onstage. It isn't as simple as you think. You mustn't stand close to anyone on the stage. Two objects together become one object in the eyes of the audience. Here's an actor's trick. Keep looking at somebody's hands. Pretty soon he'll feel like his arms are sixteen feet long. He'll fall apart trying to put them somewhere. You have to know what to do with your hands. All these things—you get to do them instinctively."

Broadway was experiencing one of its worst seasons. Of 152 plays produced fully 121 were flops. Only sixteen were rated as hits and another fifteen as moderate successess. By late August there were only six plays left running on Broadway.

The Depression was at its peak and most Americans took to cheering themselves by whistling, "Who's Afraid of the Big Bad Wolf?" The answer—everybody!

Dr. Bogart could not be relied upon for help. He had lost most of his savings, and he and Mrs. Bogart had been obliged to move from the old brownstone house to a more modest apartment in Tudor City. More and more he was drifting into the peaceful oblivion apparently provided by narcotics. Maude Humphrey demonstrated again that she was made of stronger stuff. She stood by her sick husband with a devotion that pleased and astounded Humphrey.

Mary Philips had little better luck with jobs, but together she and Humphrey managed to scrape along. When summer came, they went to Cohasset, Massachusetts, in summer stock. To forget the Depression—mental as well as financial—they both began drinking too much. Hector Pelletier, Cohasset Chief of Police, remembers the night Mary almost bit off the finger of one of his police officers when she, Humphrey, and Broderick Crawford were picked up for drinking.

When the Bogarts returned to New York, there was no work for either of them. They pooled whatever money they had for food and entertainment with friends in similar circumstances—Mary and Mel Baker, and Miriam Howell and her husband, Ralph Warren. Miriam Howell and Mary Baker were the only members of the group working. They all lived in adjoining flats in a shabby section of New York's East Side.

Mary Baker, who later became Humphrey's agent and was a close friend for many years, recalls that he was embarrassed because he didn't have a job and usually couldn't contribute to "the kitty." Humphrey was finally reduced to making pin money playing chess at the numerous "sportlands" on Sixth Avenue in the forties. For a bet of fifty cents a game he played all comers. Humphrey was both a good chess player and hungry, and he won more often than he lost.

"I'll never forget the day he came home very excited," Mrs. Baker recalled. "The manager of one arcade had offered him a dollar a game to play the public. He finally had a real job." So every day Humphrey Bogart, former Broadway juvenile, went to the arcade, where he sat in the window playing chess for money. Even though he was poor, Bogie still had expensive tastes. Lauren Bacall remembers he once told her that rather than have a doughnut and coffee for lunch, which was all he could afford in those days, he preferred skipping lunch entirely and saving enough money to go to "21" for a drink. In those days the club also used to extend almost indefinite credit to actors and many was the time, Mary Philips ruefully recalled, that Bogie ran up a huge tab.

During the first week of September, 1934, while he was at work in the arcade playing chess, Humphrey got a message to come home immediately: His father was dying. Two days later Dr. Bogart died in Humphrey's arms at the Hospital for Ruptured and Crippled in Manhattan.

Years later, Bogie was to say he never forgot his father's death. "It was only in that moment that I realized how much I really loved him and needed him and that I had never told him. Just before he died, I said, 'I love you, Father.' He heard me, because he looked at me and smiled. Then he died. He was a real gentleman. I was always sorry he couldn't have lived long enough to see me make some kind of success."

Humphrey went alone to Fresh Pond Crematory in Long Island, the only crematory in New York City at the time, to witness his father's burial.

Dr. Bogart left Humphrey about $10,000 in debts, some $35,000 in uncollected fees, and an old-fashioned ruby ring, which Humphrey put on and was to wear for the rest of his life. Humphrey assumed the responsibility of paying off his father's debts.

The air of tough self-assurance that was to characterize Bogie in later years was conspicuous by its absence then. "He was desperate," Mrs. Baker said. "He was worried about money for the first time in his life, and he didn't know which way to turn. He felt his acting career was finished, although he kept beating on producers' doors with all the other out-of-work actors."

Finally he did get a break—as a villain in *Invitation to a Murder*. Just before the show ended its run he heard that producer Arthur Hopkins was seeking an actor to portray the Dillinger-like gunman in an important new play, *The Petrified Forest*. Humphrey called the producer's office to arrange for a reading.

"We got him all fixed and sent him over to try out for the part," Mrs. Baker said. "It was a big chance and he was mighty nervous."

Robert E. Sherwood, author of the play and a friend of Humphrey's, told Hopkins he was crazy, that Humphrey would be better in another role. But when Leslie Howard, who was the star, heard Humphrey's flat world-weary voice coming from the stage at the audition, he said, "That's the man! I want him, and I'll work with him on the part."

The Petrified Forest played two weeks in Boston before opening in New York at the Broadhurst Theater on January 7, 1935, and Leslie Howard got critical raves. Humphrey wasn't even listed with the cast in the *Herald Tribune*, although critic Percy Hammond mentioned that "Humphrey Bogart and his troupe of wise cracking killers take charge and change the play from an innocent pastoral into a wicked melodrama."

Other reviewers gave Humphrey more attention. Mr. Woollcott gallantly swallowed his original opinion of Humphrey's competence. Most important, people who thought of Humphrey Bogart as only a sleek, sybaritic, stiff-shirted, and swallow-tailed smoothie began to see him as an actor of range and depth.

For his role as Duke Mantee, Humphrey wore a three-day growth of beard. Mantee's whiskers became one of the most-discussed features of the play. The New York *Post* reported that people who went to the box office asked for seats close enough to the stage to permit them to see Duke Mantee's beard.

Only one thing marred Humphrey's elation at his success: the tragic death of his boyhood friend Bill Brady, Jr., who was trapped in bed when his bungalow at Colt Neck, New Jersey, caught fire. It was the second time in his life that Humphrey could remember crying.

At the funeral Humphrey saw his old friend and mentor, Bill Brady, Sr. Mr. Brady, who was then seventy-one, put his hand on Humphrey's shoulder and said he was glad that Bill had lived to see his best friend a success. "I always knew that one day you would be a great actor," Mr. Brady said. "I pray that I will live long enough to see that happen."

Mr. Brady's wish was granted. He died in 1950 at the age of eighty-six.

Humphrey made enough money from *The Petrified Forest* to pay off all his debts (and his father's obligations) and still have a thousand dollars in the bank in a fund that he called F. Y. money—money that gave him enough security to refuse a job he didn't want.

When Warner's bought *Petrified Forest* they signed Leslie Howard and optioned Humphrey for the movie. He and Mary made the trip to Hollywood together by train, only to find when they arrived that Edward G. Robinson had been chosen to play the gangster.

Sick at heart, Humphrey remembered that Leslie Howard had promised that if the play was made into a picture he would have his original role. He also remembered that Howard was famous for keeping his promises.

He picked up the telephone and sent a cable to Scotland, where Howard was vacationing. Back to Warner's the next day came an ultimatum: Either Humphrey Bogart played the gangster or *Petrified Forest* would be made without Leslie Howard.

"If it hadn't been for him I might still be making up in New York dressing rooms," Bogart said later. "It's not for nothing my daughter was named Leslie. But even with his pushing me, I had to do fifteen tests before I was finally signed."

Although he had a $400-a-week forty-week contract, Humphrey remembered all too well his last Hollywood fiasco. He had seen too many Broadway actors "go Hollywood" only to have their contracts dropped. He and Mary lived modestly at the Garden of Allah, a group of thin-walled bungalows clustered around a pool on Sunset Boulevard. The first time playwright Arthur Kober stayed in one of those villas he was awakened in the night by a sleepy voice saying, "Would you get me a drink of water, dear?" He got up, stumbled to the bathroom, and came back with a glass of water before he realized he was alone.

The late Robert Benchley, the Garden's patron saint, lived in Bungalow 20. Another beloved character was Ben the Bellhop, who had established a firm understanding with guests. Every time he came to a villa on an errand he received a drink as well as a tip.

There was twenty-four-hour bar service, and the Garden in those early days was the center of Hollywood's social activity. The Bogarts were soon right at home, enjoying a continuous party that floated spontaneously from one bungalow to another.

Humphrey drove to the Warner's studio in a battered Chevrolet and refused to admit that he was doing more than "just passing through" Hollywood. Jaik Rosenstein, then publicity and exploitation manager of Warner Brothers Theaters, recalls the day Humphrey came into his office to do a radio show.

"He was wearing a camel's hair overcoat frayed at the cuffs and the collar," said Rosenstein. "I suggested that now that he was a star he should get himself a new coat. 'I've seen too many guys come here, make one picture, and blow themselves to new Cadillacs and big houses,' Humphrey said. 'Then they end up in hock for the rest of their lives to the studio. I'm salting my money away for my F.Y. fund.'"

Because he was so forthright in interviews, Humphrey soon became the darling of the publicity department. The dizzy mechanics of publicity enchanted him, and he started to drop into the studio publicity office to help the boys there invent stories.

He soon learned that color rather than truth most often made news. With Geoffrey Homes, press agent on the film, he began to make up stories about himself: He had inherited a railroad station from obscure relatives in France; he once donned a beard and played a bull fiddle in a small orchestra to replace a beard-wearing, bull-fiddle-playing pal who was ill; the studio gateman never recognized him; he was number one on a list of "The Ten Meanest Men in the World"; he spent two weeks incognito in jail to get in character for his role in *The Petrified Forest*. All the stories were printed.

Even in those days Humphrey felt that the Oscar awards were nonsense, so he concocted a satirical idea for giving an annual award to the best animal actor. He wanted to give the first to an actor he didn't like, but Homes persuaded him that wouldn't be suitable. Instead he gave the award to Skippy, the dog in *The Awful Truth*. The following year he awarded it to the water buffalo in *The Good Earth*. After that the ASPCA solemnly took the idea over as the Patsy Award!

Meanwhile, the picture was coming along wonderfully well. Director Archie Mayo let Humphrey play Mantee as he had on the stage, which meant he did most of his acting while sitting in a chair holding a submachine gun—a difficult feat since he had to put the characterization across without the usual help of movement. But he did have close-ups that gave him an opportunity to register heavily with the audience.

"There were only ten pages of dialogue for me, but I sat behind that tommy gun," he once said. "That is different from holding a gun up or firing from the hip in a Western. Nobody could take his eyes off Duke because they were never sure when he was going to shoot the place up with one powerful burst."

When the picture was released Humphrey was hailed as a coming new star. Richard Watts, Jr., critic for the *Herald Tribune*, wrote: ". . . and once more Humphrey Bogart provides a brilliant picture of a subnormal, bewildered and sentimental killer."

Humphrey had finally graduated from the ranks of competent juveniles and was now recognized as a major actor. At the age of thirty-six he was about to enter on a new stage of his life. Even his name was to change. From now on he would no longer be known as Humphrey. The press and public were soon to call him only Bogie, in the American style of giving nicknames to every star and politician considered truly important.

THREE

There are many people who believe that Bogart's performance as Duke Mantee was his best. Certainly no one who saw *The Petrified Forest* is likely to forget the impact of his first entrance as he burst into that dingy café.

The impact was due in large measure to what Peter Ustinov has called his "enormous presence," the unique, inexplicable characteristic of natural stars: You cannot take your eyes off them. Certainly no one in the history of the movies has made the act of smoking a cigarette a more expressive and fascinating thing to watch.

Bogart brought to the tough-guy part a new dimension. The late Jerry Wald, who produced many of Bogart's early pictures, summed up his appeal: "He was liked by audiences because he had, even in the toughest gangster roles, a pathetic quality. He always gained sympathy."

Although Bogart's Duke Mantee became a blueprint for every cinematic gangster of the era, Jack L. Warner, head of the studio that held his contract, was not particularly impressed.

Thomas E. Dewey's gangbusting in New York had inspired a wave of gangster films, and Bogart made twenty-nine of them in a row for Warner's in the three years between *The Petrified Forest* and *High Sierra*. He was a jailbird in nine of these pictures and electrocuted or hanged in eight.

The gangster lineup for films at Warner's was called Murderer's Row. The first team was headed by Jimmy Cagney, Paul Muni, John Garfield, George Raft, and Edward G. Robinson. Bogart picked up the leavings.

He complained to Warner that the gunmen he played were all the same one-dimensional characters. "You can make a card index of the lines they speak: 'Get over against the wall.' 'Get your hands up.' 'Don't make a move or I'll shoot.' "

Warner was unmoved. After all, the pictures made money and Bogart was only a $650-a-week actor, very low on the Hollywood status pole. So Bogart continued to play heavies and be a punching bag or target for the stars. In every picture he wore a kind of uniform: a blue suit, blue shirt, black or red nondescript tie, and snap-brim hat. He wore this in all the pictures—*Bullets or Ballots, San Quentin, Kid Galahad, Dead End, Racket Busters, Invisible Stripes, The Roaring Twenties, They Drive By Night*. He always wound up dead or maimed and never got the girl.

A study of his critical notices in the thirties reveals they were all good. The public and the reviewers accepted him, and Hollywood press people were delighted to have him in their midst. It was the era of sweetness and light, when the studios were trying to make the film capital and its citizens as wholesome and pallid as Pablum. Every star tried to be like the boy or girl next door. The impression given by press releases of the time was that each actor was so clean-living he ought to be running for Congress.

Bogart was the exception. He refused to pose for pictures in riding togs with "his spirited steed"; he said he wouldn't be caught dead with a pipe in his mouth fondling his favorite setter; he never let press agents suggest pleasant inanities for him to mouth at interviews.

He stubbornly refused to conform to the local mores. In an interview published in the New York *Telegraph* in 1936—just a few months after *The Petrified Forest* was released—he said he had made a careful study of "Going Hollywood," a phrase he detested. According to his statistics, 47 percent of all actors coming to the film city from the East "went Hollywood" before they had been in the film capital six months.

The public soon discovered that Humphrey Bogart in person was not detectably different from the tough, sardonic movie actor of the same name. This similarity between the screen shadow and the substance was rare enough in Hollywood during the late thirties to make Bogart the darling of the fan magazines, which were then at their peak in popularity and power. They quoted him frequently and at length, because he would tell them exactly what he thought on any given subject, with a fine disregard for conventions or consequences. In one 1937 interview he said, "I believe in speaking my mind. I don't believe in hiding anything. If you're ashamed of anything, correct it. There's nothing I won't talk about." What is most fascinating about these interviews, however, is that what he said in 1937 was just as valid twenty years later. His opinions remained the same through the years, with only minor embellishments.

"Nobody likes me on sight," he said in one particularly frank interview. "I suppose that's why I'm a heavy. There must be something about the tone of my voice, or this arrogant face—something that antagonizes everybody. I can't even get in a mild discussion that doesn't turn into an argument.

"The thing is I can't understand why people get mad. You can't live in a vacuum, and you can't have a discussion without two sides. If you don't agree with the other fellow, that's what makes it a discussion. I'd feel like a sap, starting things by throwing in with my opponent, and saying, 'Well, of course you may be right,' and 'You know more about it than I do,' and all the other half-baked compromises the tact-and-diplomacy boys use.

"My idea of honest discussion (maybe the word is argument) is to begin by declaring my opinion. Then, when the other fellow says, 'Why, you're nothing but a GD Fool!' things begin to move and we can get somewhere. Or, I'm the one who pulls that line on him. Anyway, it gets a lot of action.

"All over Hollywood they are continually advising me, 'Oh, you mustn't say that. That'll get you in a lot of trouble,' when I remark that some picture or director or writer or producer is no good. I don't get it. If he or it isn't any good, why can't you say so? If more people would mention it, pretty soon it might have some effect. This local idea that anyone making a thousand dollars a week is sacred and beyond the realm of criticism never strikes me as particularly sound reasoning."

When a columnist stated that Bogart "refuses to conform to Hollywood standards of behavior," he retorted, in a 1937 interview:

Why can't you be yourself, do your job, be your role at the studio and yourself at home, and not have to belong to the glitter-and-glamour group? Actors are always publicized as having a beautiful courtesy. I haven't. I'm the most impo-

lite person in the world. It's thoughtlessness. If I start to be
polite you can hear it for forty miles. I never think to light
a lady's cigarette. Sometimes I rise when a lady leaves the
room. If I open a door for a lady, my arm always gets in the
way so that she either has to duck under or get hit in the
nose. It's an effort for me to do things people believe should
"be done." I don't see why I should conform to Mrs. Emily
Post, not because I'm an actor and believe that being an actor
gives me special dispensations to be "different," but because
I'm a human being with a pattern of my own and the right
to work out my pattern in my own way.

If I feel like going to the Trocadero wearing this coat (a
particularly shabby brown-checked jacket with suede patches
at the elbows) and a pair of moccasins, that is the way I go
to the Troc, if at all. If I go to the Troc and want to make a
jackass of myself in front of every producer in town, that's
my business.

I really can't understand why actors can't have human
frailties like other people; why they can't make the same
mistakes, guess wrong now and then; why they must be presented to the world as of a uniform and unassailable virtue.

I'm not popular in the hail-fellow-well-met sense in which
the phrase is meant. I'm not like Frank McHugh who has to
shake his pals off his coat lapels. I have a few good, close
friends, that's all. Everybody doesn't like me. And I don't
like everybody.

The actor is supposed to be a "man's man." It's doubtful
whether I'd qualify or not. I don't hunt big game or mice,
because I don't like to kill things. I don't fish because I fished
for ten years and never caught anything. So that lets me out
of the man's man class.

I like to talk when I have stimulating people around me,
but not for the sake of hearing my own jaws clatter. I'm a
liberal Democrat and think Roosevelt's a grand guy.

I want to be comfortable but not in any super fashion. I
don't need a yacht, a swimming pool, a private projection
room, a deluxe car. I only want the things I need for my
comfort: a pleasant home, a good car, some kind of boat to
bat around in.

I'm not a respecter of tradition, of the kind that makes
people kowtow to some young pipsqueak because he is the
descendant of a long line.

I take my work seriously, but none of this art for art's
sake. Any art or any job of work that's any good at all sells.
If it's worth selling, it's worth buying. I have no sentimentality about such matters. If someone offers me five dollars
a year more than I'm getting I take it. And I would kiss an
"old stand" good-by without a single tear drop.

I believe in the institution of marriage. The institution is right, it's the human beings who are wrong. I believe in love, but not "the one love of a lifetime," as pretty a tale as that always makes. There couldn't be just one love—among fifty million people that would be pretty hard to find.

Love is very warming, heartening, enjoyable, a necessary exercise for the heart and soul and intelligence. If you're not in love, you dry up. I am in love now. After all, the best proof a man can give of his belief in love and marriage is to marry more than once. If you're not married or in love you're on the loose and that's not comfortable. Love is comforting, too. It is the one emotion which can relieve, as much as is ever possible, the awful, essential loneliness of us all.

At the time, Bogart and Mary Philips were having domestic problems. Mary had come to Hollywood with him, but she was restless while he was working. There was nothing for her to do in films. She felt her career was on Broadway.

When she got an offer to go back to New York to do *The Postman Always Rings Twice*, she accepted it. Bogart was furious.

"This is the first time I've really been able to support you," he said. "We could never afford to have children before. Stay here and let's start a family. Anyway, the play isn't any good and you're wrong for it."

Mary, however, was determined to return to New York. Bogart was right—the play wasn't good and Mary was wrong for it, but she stayed looking for work. And like most human relationships, their marriage was not improved by the long separations.

Meanwhile, Bogart had met another girl, a hard-drinking, bosomy blonde named Mayo Methot, who was in the process of getting her second divorce. The daughter of a sea captain on the Orient run and an Oregon newspaperwoman, Mayo had been in show business since she was a child. She played summer stock in Portland, then went to Broadway, where she made a reputation opposite George M. Cohan in *The Song and Dance Man* and later enhanced it in *Great Day*.

Although he had met Mayo in New York, Bogart wasn't particularly interested in her until the night of the annual dinner of the Screen Actors Guild at the Biltmore Hotel in downtown Los Angeles. Mayo was strikingly attractive in a flaming red dress with a conspicuous décolleté.

Bogart was sitting with a table of friends when he saw Mayo smile at him from the balcony. Suddenly, he remembered that he knew her from New York. Tipsily, he wrested the figure of a nude woman off a pillar and presented it to Mayo as an "Oscar for being the most beautiful woman in the room." They danced, and later that night, after her date dropped her off at her apartment, Bogart came by for a drink. After that they saw each other frequently.

Bogart had gotten a good buy on a 36-foot cruiser that he kept at Newport Beach, where he joined the yacht club. Mayo also loved the sea, and they began spending their weekends there. Finally, Mayo moved into his bungalow at the Garden of Allah.

That was the situation Mary Philips confronted on her next visit to Hollywood. Bogart didn't want to marry Mayo, but Mary insisted on his deciding between her and Mayo. The situation ended as one might predict—in disaster.

Mary said she was going back to New York to get a divorce. Bogart, neatly trapped, suddenly found himself en route to the altar again. He had belatedly discovered that Mayo was jealous of every woman he worked with in a film. Worse, she showed unmistakable signs of being an alcoholic. But there was no decent way out. In a rather revealing interview he explained why he was marrying for the third time.

I like a jealous wife. I can be a jealous husband, too. Mayo's a grand girl. She knows how to handle me. She says —and she has an idea there though the thing started out as a joke—that men watch their step with other men because they're afraid of being asked to step outside. When I go to a party and the party spirit gets at me I'm apt to flirt with any amusing girl I see. But I don't mean it. My wife's job, and Mayo has promised to take it on, is to yank me out of the fire before I get burned.

Another reason why we get on so well together is that we don't have illusions about each other. We know just what we're getting, so there can't be any complaints on that score after we're married. Illusions are no good in marriage.

And I love a good fight. So does Mayo. We have some first-rate battles. Both of us are actors, so fights are easy to start. Actors always see the dramatic quality of a situation more easily than other people and can't resist dramatizing it further. For instance, I come in from a game of golf. Maybe I've been off my drive. I slump into a chair. "Gosh, I feel low today," I start. She nods meaningly. "Low, hmm. I see. You feel low. You come to see me and it makes you feel low. All the thrill has gone and—you feel low." And we go right on from there. We both understand that one of the important things to master in marriage is the technique of a quarrel.

On August 20, 1938, a few days after his divorce from Mary Philips was final, Bogart and Mayo Methot were married. He was thirty-eight, she was thirty-five. The ceremony and reception held at Mary and Mel Baker's house in Beverly Hills was a suitable trailer for the future of this turbulent marriage.

The entire Warner Brothers police department was on hand to keep uninvited guests from attending. Mrs. Walter Abel played the harp and Judge Ben Lindsay performed the simple service. Then a reception was held in the garden, where dozens of tables with white napery, silver service, and bouquets of flowers had been arranged in the form of a huge U so everyone could be served easily. Food and a flood of champagne and whiskey were served by a corps of waiters.

Mrs. Baker recalls that Mischa Auer, the famous mustachioed Russian character actor, was on her left. Suddenly he disappeared.

"The next thing I saw was Mischa standing in the center of the U—stark naked and doing a Cossack dance. I thought Judge Lindsay was going to have a stroke. The other guests just accepted it—it was that kind of party!

"The wedding night was equally unconventional. Mayo and Bogie had one of their usual fights, so Bogie and my husband went off to get drunk. Mayo spent the night with me."

Bogart bought a house on Horn Avenue over the Sunset Strip, complete with twenty-one finches, five canaries, four dogs, four cats, and a garden featuring sweet peas and petunias, which he tended himself. In such peaceful surroundings he and Mayo began to perfect the technique of the marital quarrel.

Jaik Rosenstein, who was present at the inception of many family disputes, recalls that they could start without notice or seeming provocation. "Mayo resented Bogart's growing popularity and the fact that she gave up her career to be just Mrs. Bogart," he said. "And the resentment was always showing. Bogie would come into the house after work and say to her, 'Boy, it was hot. All day.'

"Mayo would sneer, 'Well, well. Get the great big star. *It was hot all day,* he says. Why don't we call the Associated Press and advise the world by teletype, *Mr. Bogart, the great big Warner Brothers star, says it was hot today. Flash!'*

"Then," said Rosenstein, "the fireworks would begin."

They soon became known in the press as "The Battling Bogarts," and their home had a sign out front: Sluggy Hollow. Their boat was called *Sluggy* after his pet name for her. Even their Scotty dog was named Sluggy.

Parties at Sluggy Hollow might start off decorously enough, but usually they disintegrated into a battle. Not infrequently the guests, infected with the Bogarts' brawling, joined in the fray, and more than one party ended in a free-for-all.

At a New Year's Eve party at their home, attended by James Thurber, Elliot Nugent, Louis Bromfield, and other celebrities, the marital spirit was such that one bespectacled guest challenged another: "Let's fight with our glasses on." Thurber was so fascinated that he sent the Bogarts a window-sized cartoon of the fracas inscribed "Jolly Times—1939" that Bogart hung over the mantel of the bar.

It is a cliché in psychology that people frequently choose a partner in marriage who has characteristics that they admire but lack themselves. Mayo was truly tough: She was a tiger who would take on anyone in a fight, whereas Bogart was by background a gentleman and not at all a violent man. He enjoyed a noisy argument but not slugging it out.

"Bogart was never a tough guy," confirms Mary Baker. "The only time he was tough was when Mayo forced him to be. Invariably she picked a fight and when she did he fought back. He got so used to bottles being thrown at him at home that the violence of a movie fight scene seemed tame to him."

Sometimes when he and Mayo were in the midst of one of their brawls she would suddenly pick up her highball and heave at him. Bogart never bothered to duck, but would sit calmly in his chair while the glass whizzed uncomfortably close to his face. "Mayo's a lousy shot," he would explain to guests as the glass shattered behind his head. "I live dangerously. I'm colorful. But Sluggy's crazy about me because she knows I'm braver than George Raft or Edward G. Robinson."

Instead of trying to hush stories about his militant marital life, Bogart related funny anecdotes to anyone who interviewed him. He told reporter George Frazier about the night he and Mayo were emerging from "21" in Manhattan and were besieged by autograph hounds.

"In his anxiety to get away, Bogart slammed a taxi door just as his wife was about to step in," Frazier reported. "The awareness that she was surrounded by a gibbering mob of her husband's admirers increased her anger. 'That cheap little ham actor,' she screamed, going on in such a vein for two or three minutes. The kids listened in awe. Finally, one youngster closed his autograph book and turned to his companion to say, in a voice quivering with admiration, 'Gee, she's even tougher than he is.' "

There were, however, a few stories Bogart never told the press. For example, he always knew when Mayo had crossed the line from pleasant drunkenness to hostility: She started to sing "Embraceable You." It was her battle hymn, her theme song for "Look out!" She sang it the night she stabbed him with a butcher knife.

Bogart liked to go to the Finlandia Baths on Sunset Boulevard occasionally to dry out, to rest away from her. She resented his being away, enjoying himself without her, so she decided that the baths were really a whorehouse.

On this night when he came home from the baths Mayo was waiting in the living room for him, her eyes puffy and glazed. She was humming "Embraceable You" so he knew he was in for it. But she didn't say a word. Instead, she lunged at him with the knife. He ducked and tried to run for the door. Somehow she stabbed him in the middle of the back.

Bogart fell to the floor and passed out. When he came to Mary Baker was there yelling, "Don't pull the knife out! I'll get a doctor."

He passed out again and revived in time to hear a doctor say, "It's not so bad. Only the tip went in. He's a lucky man."

He heard Mary say, "Remember, doctor, no publicity about this. We agreed on that, didn't we? You won't say a thing?"

It cost $500 to find a doctor who would keep it under his hat—a hundred dollars a stitch—but Mary did it.

Mayo smothered him with kisses the way she always did after a particularly bad fight. When he didn't respond because the pain was too great she accused him of coming home tired because of "those girls at the bath." She was going down to Finlandia to tear the place apart, but Mary, who was still there, quieted her down.

Mary Baker, the only woman Mayo wasn't jealous of, always turned up in Bogart's life when she was needed. One drunken night Mayo set fire to the house. While he was in the dining room battling the blaze Mayo was on the telephone to Mary. "Call the fire department damn it," he yelled.

But Mayo, loaded as she was, had the sense to call Mary first.

"Come right away," she said to Mary, "I just set fire to the house."

Mary didn't ask any questions, but within minutes the chief of the Warner Brothers studio police was at the door. He beat the fire department there and took charge. Again there wasn't any publicity.

Mayo also was able to drink most men under the table, a feat Bogart greatly admired. From a moderate drinker he became during their marriage a steady and capacious one, though never a lush.

Pat O'Moore, an actor friend of Bogart's, said it was through drinking with Bogart that he realized there was something wrong with his own drinking.

"I thought we drank the same, but I noticed that Bogart was still cold sober at the end of the evening and I wasn't," he said. "I said to him one day down at the boat, 'There's something wrong with my drinking, Bogie. I don't know what it is, but you can be all right when you want to be and I can't.' He said, 'Well, kid, you don't handle it right. You've crossed the line.'"

Nunnally Johnson, the writer-producer, one of Bogart's friends on Broadway, believed that Bogart was one of those favored men born with "alcoholic thermostats" in their foreheads that enable them to drink with pleasant and stimulating results, never slopping over.

"Bogart just set his thermostat at noon, pumped in some Scotch and stayed at a nice even glow all day, automatically redosing as necessary," Johnson said.

Bogart developed an affinity for Scotch through his friendship with Mark Hellinger. "Mark introduced me to Scotch," he said, "and it is a very valuable part of my life. Once I drank most anything. Then Mark told me that I was drinking like a boy and he was right."

One thing Bogart also learned from Hellinger about Scotch was when to stop drinking it. Hellinger always tried to drink him under the table, but Bogart would have none of it.

"He tried to ruin me," Bogart said. "I finally told him, 'Look, old boy. I surrender.' I don't believe this business of drinking anybody under the table is an accomplishment. Drinking is not a matter of being strong. Some people have a head for it, and some don't."

He was the only actor since the martini-loading W. C.

1. Bogie at the age of two, when his sister Pat, christened Frances, was born.

2. Humphrey at eight.

3. After Humphrey left Andover in 1918, he enlisted in the navy and was assigned to the troop transport, *Leviathan*.

4. Bogie's first wife, actress Helen Menken, whom he married on
May 20, 1926, in New York City.

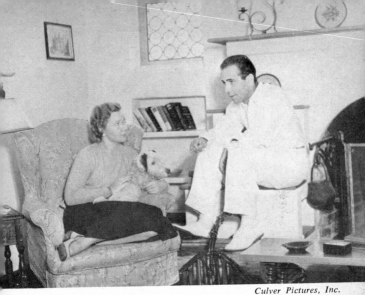

5. Humphrey and his second wife, actress Mary Philips.

6. Humphrey and his third wife, Mayo Methot.

Culver Pictures, Inc.

7. In his early days at the studio Warner's tried to develop Bogie's public image.

8. Bogie off-screen.

Wide World Photos

9. Humphrey and novelist Louis Bromfield look on as Betty cuts her wedding cake, May 21, 1945.

Wide World Photos

10. "If you want anything just whistle."

Wide World Photos

11. The Bogarts were in the forefront of some twenty-five people who protested Congressional investigation of Communists in the motion picture industry.

12. On the set of *Key Largo.*

Wide World Photos

13. Life with father.

14. When Betty was pregnant with Leslie, Bogie was fifty-four.

Phil Stern

15. Bogie and Leslie.

16. The Bogart home in Holmby Hills.

Wide World Photos

17. Stephen, Leslie, and Betty.

Phil Stern

18. The children on the set.

Dennis Stock

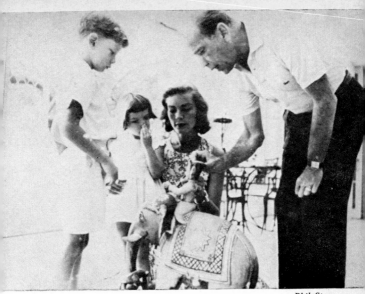

Phil Stern

19. Bogie shows off a new toy elephant.

20. The Rat Pack.

21. Karl Malden, Greer Garson, and Humphrey accept 1951 Oscars.

John Swope

22. Bogie at the helm of the *Santana*, his fifty-five-foot sailing yacht.

23. Bogie with his good friend, restaurateur Mike Romanoff.

Globe Photos

24. Bogie's dream was that one day his son, Stephen, would have as much respect and affection for the sea as he had.

Fields who did not try to conceal from the public the fact that he drank whiskey and lots of it. "Something happens to people who drink," he once said. "They live longer."

Pat O'Moore has suggested that Bogart drank because there was a streak of insanity in him, and the alcohol saved his sanity. "There came a time when the pressure built up inside and he had to drink," O'Moore said. "I used to see him so frustrated with anger that he would sit and quiver all over." O'Moore also believed that Bogart drank to spite people like Jack L. Warner.

Bogart's own attitude about the benefits of alcohol is best expressed by what he said some years later: "The whole world is three drinks behind. If everybody in the world would take three drinks, we would have no trouble. Of course it should be handled in moderation. You should be able to handle it. I don't think it should handle you. But that's what the world needs—three more drinks."

Mayo, however, did not believe in moderation. She could and did drink until she was unable to stand, and Bogie claimed she did her best to get him to increase his consumption. "She got me drinking and kept me drinking because that was the only way she felt she could keep me," he once said.

But Bogart seemed to thrive on their battles. People who witnessed their wrangling are fairly well agreed that he took pleasure in goading his wife. He was even proud of Mayo's fiery temper and ability to scrap.

In addition to the frequent public marital scraps, Bogie's image as a tough guy occasionally attracted the same kind of idiot who takes a swing at a prizefighter to prove how gutsy he is. One night in a Hollywood bistro Bogart was, in Mayo's estimation, bothered by such a heckler for far too long. She stepped between her husband and the offending party and floored the heckler with one superb punch. Bogart grinned, grabbed his wife's arm and, holding it aloft, addressed the ringside: "She's marvelous. I wouldn't go anywhere without her."

Another evening, when Bogie and Mayo were sitting in the taproom of a New York hotel having a nightcap before retiring, a man stopped at their table and leaned over so close his face was inches away from Bogart's.

"They tell me you're a tough guy," said the stranger. "Well, you don't look so tough to me."

Bogart knew what not to do. He had learned that before.

"Sit down, chum, and have a drink," he said grinning amiably.

"Okay, Bogart, I will," said the stranger, ordering a rye and ginger ale. "I hear you don't like to sign autographs for kids, that you brush them off because you want to be tough all the time. Is that right, Bogart?"

Bogie turned to Mayo. "Honey, you look a little tired," he said. "Don't you think we'd better go up and turn in?"

But this time the stranger had Bogart by the arm. "Just what I thought," he said. "Trying to run out. Tough, eh? That's a laugh."

The man was not drunk, and Bogart knew it. He just wanted to be able to tell the boys next day how he had told off "the tough movie actor."

It was a difficult spot for Bogart, who was beginning to get enough of the belligerent guest. He started to get up when the stranger uncorked a right. It landed high and did no damage, but the battle was on.

The men clinched and wound up rolling on the floor. Mayo quickly removed her shoe and beat a tattoo on the stranger's head with the heel. The Bogart family was on the way to a clear-cut decision when the management stepped in and stopped the brawl.

Later, in the elevator, Mayo turned to her husband to say, "Darling, it must be wonderful to be a movie star and receive such recognition from your fans."

It would be unfair, however, to assume that Bogart's marital life was an unending battle and that Mayo was only a fiery-tempered, drunken shrew. "They both liked to fight because the more vigorous the battle the more vigorous their lovemaking after it," Pat O'Moore said. "Their marriage was kept together because of the fighting, their fantastic physical attraction for each other, and their love of sailing."

Also Mayo was remarkably kind to Bogart's mother, who had come to live with them, and to Frances Rose (Pat), his sister, who had suffered a nervous breakdown in New York and moved to an apartment near them in Hollywood. Bogart's other sister, Catherine, had died in 1937, at the age of thirty-three. "She was a victim of the speakeasy era," Bogart explained to friends. "She burned the candle at both ends, then decided to burn it in the middle." The record shows that Catherine died on the operating table of a ruptured appendix. Excessive drinking had weakened her resistance, the medical history said.

When Bogie's mother died of cancer in Hollywood at the age of seventy-five, Mayo took over the funeral arrangements. And it was Mayo who was responsible for getting Bogart a business manager, Morgan Maree, who wisely invested Bogart's money and saw to it that he and Mayo lived on a budget.

One item on that budget was for a carpenter named Graham, who was on constant call. His job was to repair any damage the Bogarts might have inflicted on a host's home or in their own.

Patrick O'Moore recalls a night when he and his wife had dinner at the Bogarts' with comedy writer Mel Baker, Mary's husband. "Mayo came into the room just at a moment when all conversation had died. She instantly decided we must have been talking about her.

" 'Why you goddam sons of bitches, I know you were cutting me up,' she said, and rushed upstairs.

"We sat down to dinner without her. May Smith, the cook, came in and started serving when suddenly we heard the boom of a .45 revolver going off upstairs.

"We all looked up, then at Bogart. 'Forget it,' he said.

"A little while later there was another shot.

" 'We'd better go upstairs,' said Bogart.

"We went up to their bedroom which was off the balcony and Bogart banged on the locked door. 'Mayo, open it up or I'll smash it in,' Bogart said.

" 'Get away from that door or I'll plug you,' shouted Mayo.

"Bogart smashed the door down and went in. Mayo was lying on the bed crying.

"When Bogart finally came downstairs I asked him where in the hell he was going to get another door. 'Easily,' he said and took me down into the cellar. There were twelve doors there. Bogart said they put a new door in at the rate of one every other week.

"During those days Bogart would come to Warner Brothers with bags under his eyes a redcap couldn't have hefted. I stayed with him sometimes at a hotel when Mayo would kick him out of the house. Every morning he would light a cigarette on awakening, order orange juice and coffee. Then we'd go down to the car and he'd be sick for a few minutes. After he vomited, we'd go to the studio and he'd have more coffee. Then he'd be all right."

Bogart revealed none of this tempestuous life before the

cameras, but consistently turned in smooth, underplayed, professional characterizations of cheap villains in pictures by no means worthy of his talent. He was fighting on all fronts: on the screen, at home with Mayo, and at the studio with Jack L. Warner, who finally recognized his popularity as a heavy but never considered him for better roles.

"I'd read a movie script and yell that it was not right for me," Bogart once explained. "I'd be called for wardrobe and refuse to report. Jack Warner would phone and say, 'Be a good sport.' I'd argue and say 'no.' Then I'd get a letter from the Warner Brothers lawyers ordering me to report. I'd refuse. Then another wire from Warner saying that if I did not report he'd cut my throat. He'd always sign it, 'Love to Mayo.' "

Bogart's answer would be as short and sharp, ending "Love to Ann [Mrs. Warner]." But usually he lost these battles and ended up doing his best in a bad picture.

In 1940, thanks to a fortuitous chain of circumstances, he got an important break. George Raft had been offered the role of a gangster in a picture called *High Sierra*. The Hollywood censors decreed that the gangster must die, because he had committed six killings. Raft refused to die in a film. Paul Muni turned it down because it had been offered first to Raft. Cagney declined it, and so did Edward G. Robinson.

Warner had no alternative but to heed the advice of Charles Einfeld, his publicity director, and assign the role to Bogart. When Mary Baker, who was then a partner with Sam Jaffe, called to say the studio wanted him to do the film Bogart said, "Sure. Where the hell's the script and when do I start?"

The script was delivered to him Thursday morning as he was leaving for a weekend of sailing with the Coast Guard. A junior commander of Flotilla #21, Bogart attended weekly classes and stood watch when called on to relieve enlisted personnel. It was a long weekend for him but he was ready for work, script memorized letter-perfect, on Monday morning.

Although the film was an old-style gangster melodrama Bogart brought to the part of the killer, Roy Earle, a psychopathic ferocity combined with an appealing naïveté. In reviewing the picture the *Herald Tribune*'s Howard Barnes wrote: "Humphrey Bogart was a perfect choice to play the role. Always a fine actor, he is particularly splendid as a farm boy turned outlaw, who is shocked and hurt when newspapers refer to him as a mad dog. His steady portrayal is what makes the melodrama something more than merely exciting."

Bogart went to New York with Mayo and Mary Baker to make some public appearances for the picture's opening. On the first day they found they literally could not leave the stage door—the street was jammed with Bogart fans. They had to move from the Algonquin Hotel and live in a dressing room in the theater to avoid the crowds.

But Warner still refused to believe that Bogart had any sex appeal. "He's a tough guy, not a lady's man," the great man decreed.

Once again George Raft inadvertently furthered Bogart's career when he refused a role in *The Maltese Falcon* because he would not entrust his talent to an untried director named John Huston.

The Maltese Falcon, by Dashiell Hammett, established a whole new genre of detective stories—cool, downplayed, explosively violent, the chief character of whom is an admirable but tragic antihero. In the story an arrogant private operative sends his partner out to trail a possible killer. The partner gets killed, and before the complex plot is unraveled there are two more murders, numerous sluggings, and a brutally realistic romance that culminates when the detective sends the woman to the penitentiary. Hammett, who had been a detective himself, wrote the melodrama with convincing realism, and Huston's direction captures that sense on film.

Bogart's chilling but somehow engaging characterization of the private eye, Sam Spade, was much the same as his gangster roles, except he changed his dark, well-cut overcoat for a trench coat. His gravelly voice and intense manner were perfectly suited to the role of a private detective living by his wits and Huston had him dominating nearly every scene. Bogart delivered such lines as, "Sorry, angel, I have a pressing date with a fat man," with an offhand nonchalance that made one aware of both his sex appeal and his disillusion with love.

The others in the film were also excellent. Sydney Greenstreet played the "Fat Man," head of an international gang, with bland villainy. Peter Lorre, who was to become one of Bogart's closest friends, played an effeminate scoundrel who was the Fat Man's shadow.

But it was Bogart who stole the show. Richard Shickel, in his discussion of Bogart in *The Stars*, summed up the appeal he had in roles like Sam Spade: "The central fact of his existence was loneliness shaded by desperation and accompanied by that special kind of unshaven squalor that is the mark of bachelorhood in a modern American city—unscraped dishes in the sink, rye whiskey in the file drawer of the desk, a magazine resting on an ottoman in front of the worn but comfortable easy chair commanding views of the television set and the bedroom of the pretty girl who lives across the airshaft and draws the shades carelessly when she undresses.

"His special knowledge was of the jungle of the city at night—which clubs the syndicate ran, which one-arm restaurants served good coffee, which hotels a whore could use, which streets were safe to walk upon after midnight. It was this detailed knowledge that set Bogart apart from the ordinary lonely male; it was the rightness of the setting, mood and dialogue that established empathy with him."

Bogart was tough and self-reliant, but through this facade audiences sensed that somehow, somewhere in his past he had been exposed to Class. "They were constantly flattered by the revelation that a sudden call to dine with a jewel importer at the Ritz would find him shaved and dapper, handling the silverware properly, unawed by the wine list," said Alistair Cooke.

When *The Maltese Falcon* was finished Bogart and Mayo went to New York for a short vacation. Geoffrey Homes, who had been the press agent on *The Petrified Forest*, was then living on West 56th Street. There was a rap on his door late one snowy winter night. It was Bogart with two bottles of Scotch under one arm, a chessboard under the other, and a battered prizefighter at his heels.

"Mayo's mad at me," explained Bogart. "She doesn't like prizefighters."

He and Homes drank the Scotch and played chess, and the prizefighter went to sleep. Then they decided something should be done about Mayo, presumably wandering lonely in the snowstorm. She wasn't at "21," where they solemnly toasted her a few times. She wasn't at the Stork Club, where they had another blast. She wasn't in Bleeck's, where they ran into Dick Watts and Howard Barnes and Stanley Walker of the *Herald Tribune* and stayed for a few drinks.

Then they decided it was too cold to look for Mayo any more. Instead they would write a play. They started one about a saloon in Stockholm run by a slattern with an idiot son who sat through the whole performance with a spittoon in his lap. In the second act a girl came downstairs carrying a man's head under her arm.

"No use," Bogart decided. "It's too grim. Let's write a mystery about a guy living on a barge who finds a dead woman with a butterfly tattooed on the sole of her left foot and a thousand-dollar Confederate bill in her purse."

They continued on to a couple of other places. Bogie bought a big stuffed Scotty dog as a peace present for Mayo. They took the dog to the Algonquin Hotel, where he and Mayo were staying. Mayo wasn't in the suite.

"That's gratitude for you," said Bogart. "I bring home a beautiful dog and what happens. She isn't home. I won't stay here."

He got another suite. In the morning he found that Mayo had also come back to the room and found it empty. In high dudgeon she had taken another suite on the floor above. She was awakened the next day by the maid pushing the stuffed dog into her bedroom.

Then she went in search of Bogart and the battle reopened —this time over the expense of the three suites. Eventually they framed the receipted bill for breakage as a souvenir of their stay at the Algonquin. It was hung over the mantel of their Hollywood home, alongside the Thurber cartoon.

While in New York, Bogart took time out for some other capers. He gave an interview in which he referred to Jack L. Warner as a creep. Warner called him from Hollywood the next day. "How dare you call me that?" the studio chief demanded. "The dictionary says that a creep is a loathsome, crawling thing."

Bogart retorted: "I spell it kreep with a *k*, not creep with a *c*."

"But how can you do this to me?" Warner asked. "You know how much I love you."

"I did it for publicity—for the studio and you," Bogart explained.

When he got back to Hollywood, Bogart went to see Jack Warner to apologize. Warner was delighted by having a star come to him, even though Bogart considered the apology as part of the game. The late Peter Lorre once recalled that Bogart made it a kind of ritual to apologize to Warner.

"He'd apologize when there wasn't anything to apologize for," Lorre said. "No matter how bad a hangover Bogie had he'd always be on time, knowing his lines when it came to a shot on the set. One night we'd been out drinking all night and hadn't been in bed. For Bogie's puss that didn't matter and we went directly to the studio.

"This particular morning Bogie said, 'I want to go to Jack and explain'—he had to relieve his bad conscience. So he went to Warner and said he'd never do it again. And he didn't —until the next night."

Lorre witnessed many of Bogart's battles with Mayo, and on at least one occasion he was the catalyst who got the fight going. One night he made a bet with Charles Lederer, the screenwriter, that he could make Mayo and Bogie have a tremendous fight within minutes, starting from scratch.

Lorre invited Mayo, Bogie, and Lederer to his house. As he was walking through the bar carrying some drinks, Lorre murmured more or less to himself, "General MacArthur." That was all he said. In no time Bogart was hitting Mayo over the head with a glass and she was biting and scratching him. She was for MacArthur and he was violently against him.

Bogart finally left the house and disappeared into the night, where he began making the rounds of the bars. At 6 A.M. Lorre got a phone call. "Pick me up and take me to the studio," Bogie said, giving Lorre an address only a couple of blocks away in the Hollywood Hills. It was a private house and, on the way to the studio, Lorre heard the story.

After all the joints had closed, Bogie walked around in the Hills until he came to a house with lights on. He smelled coffee. Putting his face up against the lit kitchen window he asked for a cup of coffee. The woman inside shrieked, then recognized him and invited him in for breakfast. Then she awakened her children to join them.

Her husband was on night duty at the Lockheed plant and due about then, too. When he arrived she said casually, "Bill, Humphrey Bogart dropped in for breakfast."

Bogart learned the woman was a movie fan and invited her to have lunch with him and Jerry Wald and tour the studio the next day. Wald asked her how she knew it was Bogart when she looked through her kitchen window.

"Oh, I knew him right off," she said. "He always needs a shave."

FOUR

World War II killed the gangster film. "One gangster gunning down half a dozen men was pale stuff when Hitler was acting out scripts more brutal and obscene than anything dreamed of by Chicago's North Siders or the Warner Brothers," noted Alistair Cooke.

For the new wave of war films Cagney was too bouncy, Robinson was becoming too much a father figure, and Raft was too stylized to be pitted with any degree of realism against our enemies. Bogart was the only Warner star who could conceivably outwit a Nazi or Jap and survive, because his basic character was more adaptable than that of the other members of the screen underworld.

Although aware of his own and the world's weaknesses, he was brave when he had to be. Like our nation, he was interested in a fight for justice or principle only when his own direct stake in the outcome was made painfully clear. He reacted with surly suspicion to any appeals to his better nature but once he was committed, we—the audience—knew we were in safe hands.

As Cooke said, "He probably had no notion, in his endless strolls across the stage drawing rooms of the Twenties, that he was being saved and soured by time to become the romantic, democratic answer to Hitler's New Order. Such calculations belong to social historians, not to their subjects. Not, certainly, to an actor who had his troubles with the bartender's tab and who was grateful to take any part for which his dark and glossy appearance qualified him. He was always content to nestle in the camouflage of any fictional

73

type that came his way, provided the manager paid him and left him to himself; a very complex man, gentle at bottom and afraid to seem so."

Cooke was commenting on Bogart as he had been. But in the forties he was just beginning to evolve the private character that would later be his trademark.

Every actor, when he sees himself in a role in which he's good, finds that some of it rubs off. But Bogart was a realist. He knew the people he played so well on the screen were far removed from his own characteristics, but he recognized the value of his new image. As a "tough guy" he could get away with his own style of big-game hunting in Hollywood. His weapons were his tongue and sharp mind. His targets were the pompous and opinionated, the proud and the pretentious. He could harass, torment, and needle them, and he had a genius for discovering their weakness. When they became wrathful or belligerent, Bogart would either turn on his undeniable charm or retreat under the protective veneer of his screen character.

In part he was, as *Time* suggested in a cover profile written by Paul O'Neill, "making a shrewd bid for publicity, and in part he was giving irascible voice to his honest hatred of the crass and phony side of motion pictures."

And in part he seemed bent, as his critics charged, on playing Humphrey Bogart in public. He had always been a non-conformist—witness wearing the derby to Trinity—but now he was able to make it a full-time affair.

Bogart liked only a few people. His closest friends were Mel and Mary Baker, Raymond and Dorothy Massey, Betty and John Reinhardt, and Patrick O'Moore and his wife, Zelda O'Neil. He admired and actually liked a few actors such as Spencer Tracy and Clifton Webb, but, by and large, he reserved his real respect for writing people like novelist Louis Bromfield, Nunnally Johnson, Harry Kurnitz, Robert and Nathaniel Benchley, Noel Coward, Mark Hellinger and Charles Butterworth.

"Bogart was not easy to know," said Nunnally Johnson. "He enjoyed shocking people. It was his method of discovering quickly what they were made of and what made them tick. 'It saves time,' he said. It was also a process of elimination. You were with him or you were against him."

Johnson recalled the first time he met Bogart. It was at Chasen's restaurant one night soon after Johnson's arrival from New York, where he had been a highly respected writer. He had come to Hollywood to write screenplays.

Bogart and Mayo dropped by his table and were introduced. "Johnson, you've got to get out of Hollywood! Get back to your writing, stop prostituting yourself in this miserable place!" said Bogart vehemently, with well-chosen adjectives in the appropriate places.

"He was high," said Johnson, "and as usual he was taking over. He knew my short stories, and in his considered opinion I should have returned to writing literature instead of writing rubbish for the screen.

"I told him to go to hell, to leave me alone and be quick about it. He stayed. We became very good friends over the years, boon companions in drinking, in debating . . . and just drinking."

These were the years when the Bogart legend was being created, when the image of the "tough guy" was being formed. Not all the legend had to do with Bogart's battling with Mayo —he scrapped on other fronts, too.

Novelist-screenwriter Charles Grayson tells of a night Bogart was evicted from one of Hollywood's flossiest nightclubs, where the loudest noise tolerated was the popping of corks. The following night Bogart wanted to return to the scene of the crime.

He arrived with Mark Hellinger and suggested that Hellinger precede him and convince the manager that Humphrey Bogart, actor and yachtsman, was a changed man and a desirable patron for the club.

When Hellinger turned on the charm he had winning ways. The manager closed his eyes, pondered the problem for a moment and said, "All right. For you, it's OK."

Hellinger smiled and turned to fetch Bogart.

He noticed a crowd gathered around Bogart's car. He hurried over. There was Bogart, noisily battling two parking lot attendants. That ended the evening.

He continued to battle bitterly, publicly as well as privately, with Jack L. Warner for better parts in better pictures and with better directors. Warner agreed to team him again with John Huston in a World War II picture called *Across the Pacific*.

Near the end of the film Bogart was supposed to break out of a room guarded by Japanese soldiers. Just as they were about to shoot the scene Huston was called urgently to the telephone.

When he came back he said, "That's it. I'm in the army."

It was arranged that another director should take over the

picture. The next day, just before he left, Huston doubled the guards around the room where Bogart was being held prisoner.

The new director arrived. "There's the scene," said Huston. The new man frowned. "But just how does Bogie break out?" he asked.

Huston grinned. "That's your problem," he said. "I'm off to the war."

Just before Bogart was to start his next picture, *Casablanca*, Mary Baker and Sam Jaffe negotiated a new seven-year contract for him with Warner's. The contract was unusual because it called for him to be paid $3,500 a week for forty weeks a year, and it was without options. The studio had to renew it every year and as long as Bogart could show up for work he would have to be paid.

When Bogart asked Warner why he had agreed to a no-option contract the studio head explained, "Because nothing can happen to your face that will hurt it a bit."

Warner was telling the truth. Bogart's hangover-gray pallor, the lip drawn even tighter over his open mouth, sharp wrinkles around his eyes, and the whiskey-scarred voice all seemed to add to his appeal, rather than detract from it.

When they started to make *Casablanca*, everyone involved, including Bogart, Mike Curtiz, the director, the Epstein brothers, who wrote it, and his costar, Ingrid Bergman, thought the picture was going to be terrible. Nevertheless, Bogie worked with the same practiced professionalism that he had brought to all his other pictures. *Casablanca* was keyed to the headlines of the day, portraying the intrigue between pro- and anti-fascist forces in North Africa before the Allied offensive. It was full of preposterous moments, but Bogart wrestled with the character of the soldier of fortune, Rick, a disillusioned democrat fighting the Axis long before the rest of his compatriots. As always, he used his own version of the Stanislavsky method to make the character seem real.

"You think it," he said. "If you think it, you'll look it. If you feel sorry, you'll look sorry." Playing a cool adventurer who was not going to tell a police interrogator (Claude Rains) why he came or what he was up to, he delivered lines that have since become classics:

"I came to Casablanca for the waters."

"But there are no waters," answered Rains.

"I was misinformed."

"Sam, I thought I told you not to play that song," he

snapped at his nightclub pianist, and filmgoers realized that here was a tough man who was vulnerable to love.

While Bogart was working in the film Mayo was on the telephone to the set constantly. She was jealous of Ingrid Bergman, certain that Bogart was in love with her. She threatened to kill him if he left her. Believing the threat a real possibility, Sam Jaffe and Mary Baker took out a $100,000 policy on Bogie, insuring their firm against the financial catastrophe his death would cause.

After *Casablanca* Bogart starred with Raymond Massey in *Action in the North Atlantic.* As always he was in fine mischievous form. One scene called for the stars' doubles to jump from the bridge of a burning tanker into the water below, which was aflame with oil.

"My double is braver than yours," Bogie said to Massey, who insisted that his double was the braver man.

The upshot of the argument was that both men did the stunt themselves. Massey burned his pants off and Bogie singed his eyebrows.

"The horrified reaction we got from the director and producer made it worthwhile," Massey told me. "Bogie was the star of the picture. If he had gotten hurt it would have cost Warner's millions of dollars."

One of the featured players in the film was Dane Clark, who had been brought in by the studio in case they had trouble with Bogart. Clark was standing by for a buildup as the "new Bogart." Bogie knew this and delighted in tormenting Clark. One day he told Clark that the front office was going to change his name to Jose O'Toole and publicize him as the Irish-South American sensation. Clark marched in to a bewildered Jack L. Warner and announced that he refused to let them do it, leaving Bogie and Massey choked with laughter.

On another occasion Bogie told Clark that Sam Levene was out to steal every scene. Then he told Levene that Dane Clark didn't like him. When the two actors met for the first time, they were like a couple of snarling bulldogs. Bogart roared with laughter, and then they caught on.

Midway through the picture Bogie had a battle with Mayo that started at dinner at Chasen's and continued at home. He finally returned and spent the rest of the night in Chasen's Turkish bath, a luxury provided by the host for favored guests.

At eight the next morning, Bogart telephoned Jerry Wald,

who was producing the picture, to ask if it were possible to shoot around him.

"Why?" asked Wald. "You're all right, aren't you? You looked fine when I saw you and Mayo at dinner last night."

"Well," said Bogart, "after dinner Mayo and I went home where we had a few words, the usual friendly argument. One thing led to another and she let fly suddenly and I didn't duck. Now, I've got a black eye. Left side."

He had a beautiful shiner, more than makeup could cover. So for two days the camera focused on his right side.

As tumultuous as such disputes were, however, the Bogarts were apparently merely limbering up for the forays they engaged in during a USO tour they made to Europe and Africa during Christmas, 1943.

On the night before they left Hollywood for New York and Europe, the Bogarts had dinner at the Cock 'n Bull Bar on Sunset Boulevard with Peter Lorre, Karen Verne, Pat O'Moore, and Russ Llewellyn, Bogart's stand-in. Lorre suggested that the boys at the front would witness a real battle when the Bogarts arrived. "As for you," he said to Mayo, "you'll come back with a Purple Heart and a black eye."

Lorre's prediction of action to come was accurate. John Huston still remembers a night in Oran while Bogie and Mayo were there. She had locked him out of her room and he systematically began to break down the door, just like the Bogart of films.

An irate colonel appeared and yelled at Bogie, "Stop that. And give me your name, rank, and serial number." Bogie, who was in USO uniform, despised colonels on sight and on principle.

"Got no name, rank, and serial number," he yelled back, "and you can go to hell."

The next day Bogart, who was a guest of the army, was compelled to apologize. He did, adding, "I didn't mean to insult the uniform. I just meant to insult you."

Bogart didn't need Mayo around to stir up action. One night he fell in with a few paratroopers—lean, taut-nerved young men who took toughness for granted. Bogart and Mayo were hard pressed to go drink-for-drink with them but survived that from long practice. The denouement came, however, when the paratroopers decided to teach Bogart the trick of rolling with the fall after making a parachute landing—they convinced him it was something he ought to know in case he ever did a film about parachutists. The scene of action was a bistro, and Bogart's practice jump was to be made from the bar and without a parachute. He leaped to the applause of the chutists, landed on his head, and knocked himself cold.

Charles Grayson recalled when the Bogarts arrived in Caserta. Bogie and Huston managed to get away from Mayo and were chinning with Ernie Pyle and a bunch of battle-weary infantrymen, a few of whom were not a little skeptical of the hot shot from Hollywood.

After much talk and a few drinks a big sergeant suddenly picked up a submachine gun and tossed it at Bogart, saying, "OK, tough guy, show us how, huh?"

Bogart caught the tommy gun and in the Duke Mantee lisp said, "Thanks, pal." Then he barked, "This is it," and pressed the trigger. To his horror a stream of bullets whammed out, narrowly missing Pyle, Huston, and Grayson.

But Bogart recovered quickly and went back into character again, eyes narrowed, mouth twisted, and teeth bared. He fired two more short bursts.

Whirling, he tossed the smoking gun back to the bug-eyed sergeant and said mildly, "Pal, I didn't know it was loaded."

Between drinks and fights Bogie and Mayo put on scores of shows for the troops. Bogie would start with a speech from *The Petrified Forest*. Then Mayo would come on with Don Cummings at the accordion and sing anything requested. Almost always the boys asked for "I'll Walk Alone" and "You'll Never Know." Whether she was asked for it or not she'd always sing "Embraceable You." Bogie would look at her then, wondering if she knew it was her battle hymn. But her face was always bland, her thought concentrated on the words.

They often performed in hospitals near the lines that were usually tents. At night a nurse would go ahead of them telling the boys they were coming, holding up a gasoline lantern so the soldiers could see their faces.

Before the trip the German radio announced that the American morale was so bad that the wicked American gangster Bogart had been sent to Africa to entertain the troops. By then his image as a tough guy had been well established, even among real tough guys. One day while driving near the front Bogart ran out of cigarettes. Jumping out of the command car he walked up to some GIs in a jeep and bummed a cigarette from them. One man recognized him and, as he lit the cigarette, leaned over to ask quietly, "How're the boys doing?"

It took Bogart a second to get it, then he said, "Okay. They're fine."

"Do you think Bugsy'll take the rap?" the GI asked.

"Yeah."

"I thought so. And Lepke? Will he burn?"

"Sure, he'll burn."

The soldier drove off in the jeep with, "Well, I'll see you around. Thanks for the news."

Later Bogie heard that the GI had been in the rackets at home. He obviously was convinced that Bogart was also crooked.

Another dramatic evidence of his public image was a letter from a girl in London. She had been through more than 300 air raids. She wrote she wished he was there, because he'd know how to face it. He was so calm and cool.

While the First World War didn't touch the emotions of the young Bogart, this war did. He never forgot one boy he saw on the trip; a kid with blue eyes who was lying in a hospital bed while a nurse was writing a letter for him to his girl. They had become engaged when he left for overseas. He was writing to her and he was worried. Should he tell her the truth: that he had lost both legs and one arm?

"It's not going to make any difference to her," Bogie said with all the conviction he could muster. "She loves you, and the only thing that matters is that you come home."

The boy's face brightened and he asked Bogie to write a P.S. on his letter.

When the Bogarts returned to Hollywood Jack L. Warner was friendlier than usual. The reason: *Casablanca* had been previewed. Audiences watching Bogart play his tender, understated love scenes with Ingrid Bergman against the tinkly background of "As Time Goes By" were suddenly aware of a quality—very much a part of his own character—that had never before come through so clearly on the screen. "They saw an approximation to the melancholy man whose wryness was the mask of an incorruptibility he mocked," Alistair Cooke wrote. Warner finally began to think of Bogart as a romantic leading man, and, thanks to an Academy Award nomination for his role in *Casablanca,* Bogart become King of the Warner lot.

But he was not a king in his home. Mayo was becoming more difficult every day. "She would love him one moment, and in the next breath she would try to kill him," Pat O'Moore said.

From a beautiful, trim blonde Mayo had become blowsy. Her face was now puffy, her skin scaly. Although she was a good cook, she stopped eating and drank almost constantly.

Bogart persuaded her to go to a physician, who reported she was an alcoholic and suggested psychiatry. The psychiatrist diagnosed her as a paranoid and schizophrenic and warned Bogart that she was capable of violence to herself or someone else. He recommended psychotherapy in a rest home, but Mayo flatly refused.

One morning soon after *Casablanca* was finished Jaik Rosenstein got a telephone call from the Warner police chief. "Bogie's wife attempted suicide last night," the chief said. "You'd better get over there, see what the problem is, and hush it up if you can."

When he arrived at the house Bogart let him in. "Did she really try to kill herself?" the press agent asked.

"Well, she cut her wrists, but not very deep," Bogart said.

Rosenstein sent Bogart off to the studio, then called to Mayo, who came downstairs weeping, with clumsy bandages on her wrists. She put her arms around Rosenstein and sobbed, "Oh, I don't know what I'm going to do. I know he's running around on me."

Rosenstein told Mayo that her jealousy was natural enough but that she was overplaying it. Bogart was not interested in any other woman at the time, but he soon might be if his home life didn't improve.

"Look," Rosenstein said, "you're the woman who's supposed to love him. A man just has to believe that his wife thinks he's great. Here's a guy who all his life wanted to be a romantic star but couldn't. He didn't have a chance. They told him he was ugly, unphotogenic. All he could ever hope to play was tough guys. Suddenly he's the great lover opposite Bergman. A hero to millions—but still a bum in his own house."

Mayo finally dried her tears and said she would try to straighten up. Rosenstein drove back to the studio, and went to Bogie's dressing room. He told him that when Mayo began needling him he should ignore it, let it go in one ear and out the other.

"That would never work in a million years," Bogart answered.

Rosenstein said he ought to try it. Bogart shook his head, meanwhile finishing his makeup at the dressing table. He ad-

justed the snap brim of his hat in the mirror and started out
for the sound stage, with Rosenstein following.

Suddenly Bogart stopped and turned around. "I want to explain something that you apparently don't understand," Bogart said. "My wife is an actress. She's a clever actress. It
just so happens that she's not working right now. But even
when an actress isn't working, she's got to have scenes to
play. And in this case I've got to give her the cues."

Bogart maintained his equanimity and patience under domestic circumstances far more trying than any a script writer
could invent. After *Action in the North Atlantic* he did *Thank
Your Lucky Stars,* followed by *Sahara,* the story of a group
of Allied soldiers who captured 500 Nazis. Colonel Reinicke,
USMC, was technical advisor on the film and the German soldiers were all Marines, part of a group training to go overseas.

When the picture was finished Bogart and Mayo gave a
small dinner party in a Hollywood restaurant for Colonel and
Mrs. Reinicke and some of the other Marines and their wives.
During dinner, Mayo suddenly started muttering, "Goddam
4-F shirking bastard." Bogart asked her quietly to stop.

"Don't tell me to shut up, you neutral 4-F creep!" Mayo
shrieked and left the table.

Bogart apologized to his guests and invited them all back to
the house for a nightcap. At the front door he paused to say,
"Mayo is here somewhere. If you say anything about her
make it complimentary. She'll come out in due time."

When the group entered the house Mayo was not in sight.
Everyone said nice things about her and raved about the
house. Then, from behind a sofa, there was a grunting and
groaning. Mayo emerged—cursing. She continued her ha-
rangue until the embarrassed guests left.

Despite his domestic problems Bogart's work habits were
well-regulated. He rose early, drove to the studio in Burbank,
and worked tirelessly until noon, when he knocked off for
lunch at the Lakeside Country Club. His lunch invariably
consisted of a bottle or two of beer, two eggs over-light, crisp
bacon, toast, and black coffee.

He never objected to an interview at lunch because, as Rosenstein said, "That meant the studio would pay the check.
His first question as we got into the car heading for Lakeside
always was, 'This is on the studio, isn't it?' "

And he remained as playful as ever. Between scenes on his
own pictures he would go set-hopping, looking for a little action, which to him meant some mental stimulation. When a

friend like Nunnally Johnson was in the studio he would visit him. The routine was always the same. "He would tease and torment me," said Johnson. "But I'm thick-skinned and so was he. After some mutual insulting we would have a good debate."

During *Passage to Marseilles* Bogart walked onto the set just as Claude Rains had to turn his head and raise one eyebrow. That was all. No dialogue. Bogart broke them up when he said in his gravelly voice, "And he gets paid $5,000 a week for doing that."

His irreverence about everything was becoming a legend. He needled others but was most devastating when talking about himself. He told reporters frankly about his "wedgies," as he termed the shoe lifts that increased his height, and glorified in pointing out his "curls," as he called his phony hairpiece.

One morning he dashed out of Boystown, his name for the makeup department, and in the doorway bumped into Madame Maria Ouspenskaya, the grande dame of the lot. Without breaking stride Bogart glanced back over his shoulder and in the friendliest of moods shouted, "Good morning. How are ya, kiddie."

Under the facade, however, Bogart was tormented by a new problem: He had fallen in love with Lauren Bacall, his leading lady in *To Have and Have Not.*

Miss Bacall, a former New York movie usherette, actress, and model, was tall, with beautiful long legs, a lovely tawny complexion, and a kind of sullen arrogance perfectly expressed by her low, throaty voice. She had been spotted on the cover of *Harper's Bazaar* by Mrs. Howard Hawks, who suggested to her husband that he test her for his film.

Bacall was born Betty Perske in New York City on September 16, 1924. She went to public school there, did some modeling as a teen-ager, and enrolled at the American Academy of Dramatic Arts, where she adopted her mother's name, Bacall.

Lauren Bacall was nineteen when Bogart met her, just beginning her career and her life. He was forty-five and certain life had passed him by. But he fell in love with all the starry-eyed dedication that, as a kid, he had felt for Pickles.

They met the day she arrived in Hollywood. "I saw your test. I think we'll have some fun working together," he said with considerable foresight.

When they started shooting the film Betty was so nervous

that she couldn't keep from shaking. "I was playing a scene with Bogie and I had to catch a box of matches he tossed me and then light a cigarette," she recalled. "My hands trembled so much I kept dropping the matches. Bogie pretended to ignore it, which was just what I needed. Even from the beginning he went out of his way to be helpful and encouraging."

Between scenes and after lunch, Bogart and Bacall used to ride their bicycles through the studio streets or sit in his or her trailer having long talks. Soon his growing affection for Lauren was being hinted at in the gossip columns. It was so obvious in their film scenes that Hawks had the film rewritten to put the emphasis on them.

Mayo telephoned the set every day when he had love scenes to play with Lauren. Her sarcasm was cutting: "Hello, lover boy. How're you doing with your daughter? She's half your age, you know."

Although his marriage to Mayo had long since been put asunder—if not in the courts then at least in the home—Bogart was worried that Mayo might do something terrible to herself or Bacall. Hedda Hopper came on the set one day to warn Betty that Mayo might drop a lamp on her.

"Everyone else was afraid of Mayo, but not Betty," Patrick O'Moore said. "Bogart was enchanted with her. I remember him telling me once, 'I don't want to break this marriage up but I like her youth, her animal-like behavior and don't-give-a-damn attitude.' I think he was fascinated by this unformed thing which he could make into the perfect wife. And she wanted to be Mrs. Bogart. I still have the piece of paper on which like any infatuated schoolgirl she wrote: 'Betty Bogart, Betty Bacall Bogart, Betty B. Bogart.' "

Betty soon earned the nickname among Bogart's friends of "The Cast." "When he wasn't coming home we'd tell Mayo he was out with 'the cast,' " Mary Baker said. At Newport Betty was called "Ladder Legs." "She had long, thin legs, and she could step on board carrying a block of ice without using the ladder," Pat O'Moore said. "She set out to learn sailing because that was Bogart's big love. Within weeks she could handle a ten-foot Dyer Dink proficiently, and she became expert at crewing."

Bogart and Betty lived dangerously during their courtship. ("She courted him as much as he courted her," said Mary Baker.) One day when Betty was on board the *Sluggy*, Mayo came to the harbor checking on them. Betty saw Mayo first, tumbled off a bunk, and hid in the head. Mayo came on board and settled down to wait for Betty, who she was certain was somewhere near. Betty waited for half an hour until Bogart returned to the boat and took Mayo off.

Bogart and Bacall were anything but discreet. One night Bogie took the *Sluggy* to the yacht club with Betty aboard and tied up alongside the dock. The next morning there was an uproar among the wives of the club managers when he and Betty came on deck because it was apparent that they had spent the night aboard. The club executives decided to ask for his resignation, but Pat O'Moore and his wife, Zelda, slipped over and went below. When the club brass came aboard they were greeted by Pat and Zelda in pajamas, and yawning conspicuously. The committee members, happy to believe that Bogie and Betty had been chaperoned, stayed just long enough to have a drink.

A few weeks later at dinner in Newport, Bogart astonished the yachting fraternity by standing up and proposing a toast to, "My fiancee—Betty Bacall—the future Mrs. Bogart." That was the first public announcement of their intention to get married. Surprisingly, it was never reported in the newspapers.

When *To Have and Have Not* was completed, Bogart and Mayo went to the *Sluggy* for a weekend to work out a separation. At two the following morning Pat O'Moore got a telephone call from Bogart.

"I've left Mayo," he said. "Call Betty and ask her to come and get me on Highway 101. I'm walking to town."

O'Moore, who did not drive, called Betty, who drove up the highway at 4 A.M. looking for Bogart. "Suddenly I saw this figure in rope-soled shoes plodding down the road," said Betty.

But Mayo was finally aware that after years of being wrongly jealous of other women, one had finally come along who was a real threat to her. She was frantic, and friends convinced Bogart that if he didn't go back to her she would kill herself, or Betty, or him—or all three. He returned home and for a few weeks tried to make the marriage work, but it was an impossible situation: living with Mayo and forced to work every day with Betty.

To Have and Have Not received excellent reviews. Critics compared it with *Casablanca*. Betty, whose big line in the movie was a hoarse, "If you want anything, all you have to do is whistle," was hailed as a new and important star.

After the film was premiered Bogie and Betty had lunch one day in New York with Moss Hart, who told Betty, "You'd better retire right now, Betty. You'll never top the reviews you got for your first picture. You can get out with glory, now."

Warner's, eager to cash in on the success of the film and the publicity about the romance between Betty and Bogart, immediately cast them together in another film, *The Big Sleep*.

In December, 1944, while he was making that picture, Bogart told Louella O. Parsons that he and Mayo had separated again. "I believe it's the right thing to do," he said. "I have told Mayo I am not coming home. She can have anything she wants if she will let me go—and I believe she is too sensible to want to hold me after six years of continual battling."

Once again friends prevailed. "I came into makeup one morning and Bogie was waiting to tell me he had gone back to Mayo," Lauren Bacall said later. " 'I had to go back,' he told me. 'I wouldn't throw a dog out in the street in her condition. I have to give her every chance.' So he went back, and I cried. What else was there to do."

Bogart gave Mayo a diamond and ruby ring for a Christmas present. Again they went to Newport and aboard the *Sluggy* to talk things over. Again he started to walk back to town and was picked up by Betty.

Bogart was certain that he loved Bacall and that she loved him. He was concerned, however, about the twenty-five-year age difference. "I don't know how the hell I got mixed up with a nineteen-year-old girl," he told Lee Gershwin at a party.

It was Peter Lorre who helped make up his mind. "It's better to have five good years than none at all," Lorre advised him.

On the night that Bogart finally signed the out-of-court settlement that ended his marriage with Mayo, he met Mary Philips, his second wife, at LaRue's restaurant on the Sunset Strip.

"He was despondent and miserable," said Miss Philips, then married to Kenneth MacKenna who had given up acting and become story editor for MGM. "The end of the marriage bothered him even though he felt he was doing the right thing."

To cheer up Bogart, Mrs. MacKenna told him she wanted to give him a gift—two china dogs that had once belonged to his mother. "He cried," Mrs. MacKenna said.

Bogart was divorced from Mayo on May 10, 1945. The hearing was in private and the decree sealed. As part of the divorce settlement Bogart gave Mayo a large sum of money plus full ownership of one of the two Safeway Stores in which he had invested. He didn't contest the divorce, which was granted on the common Hollywood grounds of "great mental suffering." In the usual Hollywood tradition, Mayo told the press, "Bogie and I are the best of friends. He is a very nice guy. It was a very pleasant marriage."

Simultaneously with the news from Las Vegas that Mayo's divorce had gone through came a request from Chicago that Bogie attend the "I Am an American Day" celebration. Turning to Betty with whom he was dining, he said casually, "Meet me in Chicago. I've got a job to do there. Then we'll go on to Louis Bromfield's and get married. Might as well kill two birds with one stone."

When it was announced that Bogart and Lauren Bacall would be married as soon as possible, the irate William Perske let it be known from his home in Charleston, South Carolina, that he considered Bogart more qualified for residence in a home for the aged than for a honeymoon with his young daughter, whom he had not seen in ten years, since divorcing Mrs. Perske.

"In my opinion," Perske told reporters, "Lauren is far too young to marry a man more than twice her age. But she's a girl with a mind of her own, and the chances are that she will marry Bogart. If the wedding happens, it sure won't be with my approval. My daughter's studio advised me to keep my trap closed, but I just felt like opening it."

Betty's mother, who had since remarried and become Mrs. Natalie Goldberg, was equally concerned about the age difference, but, she later said, she never had any doubt that the marriage would be a good one.

On May 21, 1945, Bogart and Betty were married in the spacious hallway of Louis Bromfield's home, Malabar Farm, in Ohio. The ceremony lasted just three minutes and only a few close friends were present. Bogart shed tears all through the ceremony. "He cries at weddings," Betty Bacall said. "He's very cute about it. Really," she added, "I think the words get to him."

Mayo quietly left Hollywood to go back to her mother's home in Portland, Oregon. Six years later she died alone in a motel after a long illness brought on, it was reported, by acute alcoholism.

FIVE

Lauren Bacall was twenty and Bogart was forty-five when they were married. "He married me because I was younger than he, and he felt he would be getting a new lease on life," Betty once told me in Bogie's presence.

His version was different: "I had to marry her," he said. "She chased me until I had my back to the wall. I did what any gentleman would do—I acquiesced."

"I chased him—that's a laugh," countered Betty. "He set his sights for me and wouldn't rest until I said, 'I will.' "

Such banter seemed to be an essential part of their marriage. During the twelve years they were married the Bogarts behaved toward one another much like the couple in "The Thin Man" stories. Beneath their tart repartee lay a deep tenderness—but they refused to take themselves too seriously.

Soon after they were married, Bogart gave Betty her first mink coat. She carefully spread it out on the floor of their living room, took off her shoes, and slowly, luxuriously, walked on it, saying. "I've always wanted to walk on mink."

Bogart was delighted.

Marriage required considerable adjustment from both of them. Bogart was not only a film star but a gentleman and accustomed to living like one. His cook, May Smith, had been with him since his marriage to Mayo, as had Aurilio Salazar, his handyman-gardener. Bogie had grown up with servants, whereas Betty, raised in far more modest circumstances, had lived with her mother all her life.

During the first sixteen months of their marriage the Bogarts lived at a bungalow court on the Sunset Strip. Then they bought Hedy Lamarr's home in Benedict Canyon on the outskirts of Los Angeles. At the same time they acquired a butler named Fred, reportedly Oxford-educated with a brother in the Welsh Fusileers.

Mary Baker, who was present at the Bogarts' first dinner party in the new house, recalls that Betty was trying to be very much the lady. "Fred had planned an elaborate dinner," Mrs. Baker said. "There was a great deal of silver on the table. Betty took one look and obviously didn't know where to begin. Bogie told her, 'Ask Fred. He'll tell you.'"

Mark Hellinger was so fascinated by Fred that he invited Fred to come to dinner with Bogie and Betty on his night off. Gladys Glad, Mark's wife, had to run around getting sandwiches for the butler, which Mark found amusing.

Then, at a late point in the evening, Mark asked Fred if he were a Communist. "Oh, dear, Mr. Hellinger," said Fred in his Cary Grant accent, "of course I am. I am a member of a minority group. You are a Communist, too, aren't you?"

Mark said, "Well, no."

"Oh, I thought you would be," said Fred, who went on to a discussion of the countries he thought would be the next to go Communist—including China. "I've had happy times in China," said Fred. "I loved China. A wonderful country."

"I presume you've been to Hong Kong, Shanghai and the Long Bar and that's all," said Mark, thinking to put the butler down.

"Yes, Mr. Hellinger, you do presume," said Fred, quietly scoring on Hellinger.

Betty soon learned how to manage Bogart, who had expected her to be like his other three wives—a companion for his semibachelor existence.

Before their marriage, Bogart had a well-deserved reputation as a heavy drinker. He stopped seeing most of his old drinking companions, and he cut down considerably on his drinking.

I once asked Betty how she had persuaded Bogie to do it. "I had little to do with it," she said. "Insecurity made Bogie a big drinker. When he realized he had security, emotionally as well as professionally, he found he could keep his drinking within sensible bounds.

"During his drinking days, however, and there were many of them, I learned the best way to keep him from drinking too much was never to nag at him. Instead, I used to ignore him, a trick which really bothered him. For a while he'd do everything but fall flat on his face to get me to pay him some attention.

"I knew better than to try to outdrink him or stay up with him. That would be a physical impossibility for most men, let alone a woman. Also, I never tried to bawl him out that night or the next morning. When he was hung over he was so bugged and remorseful I didn't need to say anything."

Betty never had trouble with Bogart and other women. "He never looked at another girl with interest," Swifty Lazar told me. "Actually he would run for the hills if a girl made a pass at him. I was with him many times in Las Vegas with Frank Sinatra and girls would come up, and say, 'I'll meet you later, if you like.' He was petrified. He had no ambivalence about his affection for Betty or his being married. Sometimes he'd kid around and be outrageous, but he never flirted."

Occasionally, at parties where Bogie had had too much to drink, Betty would step in and declare herself. She even told certain predatory ladies off, making it plain that she was not above causing a scene if it was necessary. "Bogie disliked scenes and had no heart for the chase anyway, so other women were never a problem," Betty told me. "When he found a girl he liked he went with her and no one else. To assure himself of her companionship he might even marry her. Unfortunately, happy marriages aren't built on the prospect of good companionship alone. They also require understanding."

And Betty understood her husband very well indeed. Like most men who marry late in life, Bogie was set in his ways. He hated any kind of change, domestic or otherwise. To get him to do the things she wanted, Betty developed a technique that he admiringly called "the art of misdirection." "It works like the old shell game," he told me. "While I'm concentrating on one shell she is maneuvering another one—and the pea ends up under a third."

Betty's system worked like this. While waiting for their son Stephen to be born, Betty decided she wanted to move into a new and larger house. Bogart, who had spent most of his life in apartments or hotels, was bitterly opposed to any elaborate establishment.

Betty knew that, and knew that getting him to move

would be a long, hard battle. So she started asking for a stainless steel stove.

"Why?" asked Bogart.

"Because I can't cook on anything but a stainless steel stove," Betty answered. "I can't eat meals that aren't cooked on one; the food tastes better on stainless stoves; they are easier to clean—and if I get one I will shut up."

Bogart gave in. The next step was obvious: The kitchen was too small for the stove, and there wasn't enough closet space. Betty started to leave brooms and pans lying around. Bogie, who was very neat and orderly, would ask why they weren't put away. "There's not enough closet room," Betty said.

Slowly she went through the rest of the house, room by room, underlining every flaw. Meanwhile she started house hunting on the sly, looking at every available house—hoping to find the perfect place, one without a defect Bogart could pounce upon as an excuse not to buy.

And every time they visited friends who had lovely homes she would drag Bogie up to the nursery and talk about the baby they were expecting and how their children were going to need room to grow up.

"You grew up in a crowded New York apartment, two rooms and a bath, and there's nothing wrong with you," Bogie would retort.

Betty would drop the subject but later in the evening would turn the conversation to the schools in the vicinity. She would mention in passing that there were no good schools in their present neighborhood, and their baby would grow up a moron.

Finally one day she found the house she was looking for— but it was in Holmby Hills, an exclusive area of the film colony where Bogie had many times said he would rather be caught dead than live.

Betty started calling friends in Holmby Hills with whom she hadn't talked in years. She and Bogie began to visit them, and she brought the subject of conversation around to the neighborhood and let them do the selling.

She was, meanwhile, getting bigger daily. She started asking Bogie when they could go from the house they owned: It was too small for more children. "There will be no more," Bogie promised.

Betty finally cajoled Bogart into going out to see the

Holmby Hills house. He wasn't interested. It was too expensive, and he was happy where he was.

Betty finally pinned him down to admitting it was the cost of the house that bothered him most. Then she dropped her trump card: She had made out a list of things she would deprive herself of to get the new house. She showed him the rugs they had bought for the present house (which had never been laid because she knew they were going to move) and said they would fit the new house. She promised to furnish very slowly and told him this was the house they could grow old in—they'd never have to move again.

The stainless steel stove was the first item of furniture moved into the Holmby Hills house. One of the two principal rooms downstairs was a white marble solarium with a glass facade that opened onto the terrace overlooking the pool. The other was a huge, pine-paneled study with a big fireplace, bookshelves up to the ceiling filled with well-read books, an equally well-used bar, plenty of comfortable chairs, and a big divan opposite a huge coffee table. This was the Bogarts' favored room for entertaining.

Bogart was proud of Betty's taste, and most of the decor in the house was of her choosing. She bought a Bernard Buffet long before he was in vogue. Bogie bought a painting once, too: a misty, blue-gray abstraction. "I bought it in Paris one morning when I had one of the worst hangovers I had ever had in my life," he said. "I was out in the streets wandering around trying to keep in motion so not to think of the hangover, and I stopped in front of a gallery and saw this picture. I thought it was a battle scene. It turns out to be a harvest."

Getting Bogart to change some of his other attitudes was not so easy. He was, for example, an ardent Democrat. Shortly before his marriage to Betty, Bogart had voiced his high regard for Franklin Delano Roosevelt over the radio. Although he was congratulated by many people for daring to speak out, he was denounced by an equally large group who felt that stars should stick to acting and not political stumping. A Hollywood trade paper editorialized that actors and actresses should keep out of political discussions, on the commercial grounds that by forcing their views they were bound to offend some of their fans and hurt their draw at the box office.

Bogie was so irked by the reaction to his campaign broadcast that he wired his old friend and brother-in-law, Stuart

Rose, who was then an editor of the *Saturday Evening Post*, saying he wanted to write a piece about why he involved himself in politics. Rose wired back: "Write it yourself. If you let any Hollywood press agent touch it I'll slam it back at you."

Bogie wrote a piece entitled "I Stuck My Neck Out." In it he said, "In searching through the denunciatory letters for a possible clue to my sin I am forced to the conclusion that it lies solely in being an actor. Actors, many of the writers seem to believe, should be seen and heard only on the screen or stage. When they voice opinions on subjects more vital than love, swimming pools and the kind of breakfast food they prefer, they're stepping out of bounds. . . .

"Most motion picture actors and actresses own homes and property, which gives them a material as well as spiritual stake in the country. They even pay taxes. All of which, to my possibly biased way of thinking, qualifies them for all the rights of free expression enjoyed by their fellow citizens. . . .

"I believe we must pay the freight in this democracy by working at it with all our intelligence, or what God gave us to pass for intelligence, to keep it a living, vital force. That, to my way of reasoning, includes voicing our considered opinions on issues of the day, even who we think should be our next President—be that individual Democrat or Republican."

For a while during the 1952 election campaign, Bogie was strong for Eisenhower, as was Betty. Together they went to Madison Square Garden to greet Ike on his return from Europe. But later, Stevenson's speeches affected Betty—so much so that she gradually switched her political allegiance to him.

Again she applied the technique of "misdirection." She kept leaving Stevenson literature around the house where Bogie would be sure to see it. She was careful to never knock Ike but kept quoting Stevenson. Bogie started to watch Stevenson on television and to study his speeches carefully, explaining, "I just want to know what the opposition is up to."

Finally he became interested in Stevenson. The changeover came the night Betty was going to greet Stevenson at the Cow Palace in San Francisco. She was pregnant again at the time and didn't ask Bogie for permission to go, which annoyed him. While she was packing he went into the bedroom and said, "You can tell them if they want me, I will go, too." Betty relayed the welcome information to the Stevenson forces and they went together. And that was at a time when it was privately murmured by some studio heads that an open embrace of Stevenson might weaken the bonds of a film contract.

"Bogie never seemed to give a damn for what people said or thought," Adlai Stevenson later told reporter Peter Bogdanovich. "And it was quite perilous in those days to be a Democrat, especially one partisan to me."

Alistair Cooke met the Bogarts on the Stevenson train. "Of course Stevenson won't win," he said.

"What?" said Bogie.

"Not a prayer, I'm afraid," said Cooke.

"Why, you son of a bitch," said Betty, "that's a fine thing to say."

"Look," said Cooke, "I'm a reporter. You're the lieutenants."

The Bogarts bet Cooke ten dollars that Stevenson would win. When they lost, Bogart paid up, though he grumbled that he didn't think Cooke should take the money. "It's a hell of a guy who bets against his own principles," he said.

Betty thinks that some of her propaganda about what a great man Stevenson was may have induced Bogie to change. "But," she said, "he was always his own man, and he made up his own mind long before most other Hollywood people dared to come out for Stevenson."

The Bogarts had not always been so politically sophisticated. When in 1947 a Federal Grand Jury indicted ten Hollywood writers as alleged Communists for refusing to answer when asked if they were members of the party, the Bogarts were in the forefront of some twenty-five Hollywood people who flew to Washington to protest against the Congressional investigation of Communists in the motion picture industry.

"We went in there green and they beat our brains out," Bogart told a *Newsweek* reporter, explaining that he thought he was defending the Bill of Rights. "But in the shuffle we became adopted by the Communists, and I ended up with my picture on the front page of *The Daily Worker*.

"I detest Communism just as any decent American does. My name will not be found on any Communist front organization nor as a sponsor of anything Communistic. That the trip was ill advised, even foolish, I am ready to admit. I am an American and very likely, like a good many of the rest of you, sometimes a foolish and impetuous American."

It was typical of Bogart, however, that once the mistake was made he was willing to admit it. "Bogart never lied," Betty told me. "The one thing he could never forgive was a lie. He said if you tell a lie your character has been damaged. If you lose character you have nothing. He always felt that no matter how much he loved me, if I had ever done anything wrong that would have been the end. He said to me always, 'If you ever meet anyone and want to take off, don't do it behind my back. Come to me and tell me. If you did anything dishonest, I'd never like you again and I never want to stop liking you.' "

This honesty between the Bogarts was, I believe, what made their marriage so successful. They always said what was on their minds, they never nursed grudges, and they were always themselves.

His marriage made no change for the better in Bogart's appearance, however. His uniform around the house was a white jump suit made of terrycloth, topped off by a weather-beaten yachting cap. His feet were invariably encased in the tasseled moccasins of the period.

He disliked dressing up, even for guests, and hated shaving. And he got away with it. One day he came home from a boat race with a three-day growth of beard. Betty, who was dressed and waiting for him to go to a party with her, said, "You can't go like that."

"Nuts," he said, "Why can't I?" So he dressed and went as he was. Not one remark was made during the entire evening about his beard.

Bogart was equally nonconforming in his attitude toward birthdays, Christmas, anniversaries, and sentiment of any kind. He termed Mother's, Father's, and Valentine's Day commercial enterprises.

"Although he was sentimental when he gave me the present it was usually with a crack meant to take the sentiment from it," Betty said. "Once he gave me a gorgeous gold cigarette case with the comment, 'Here, I'm tired of seeing all that tobacco in your bag.' "

He was equally niggardly with compliments, even to his good friends. He was very fond of Nunnally Johnson but would never say so outright. Instead he might say, when other writers were discussed, "Johnson is one hundred times a better writer than that jerk."

Once when he and Betty saw Rex Harrison in *Venus*

Unobserved, just before they flew to England, Bogart was impressed with the performance but too embarrassed to tell Harrison so in his dressing room. Instead, he wrote him a postcard on the plane congratulating him.

"He sincerely resented a public display of affection," Betty said. "On seeing it coming he would beat a hasty retreat behind his porcupine bristles with such phrases as, 'Don't be mawkish' or 'Come on, grow up.' He proved his love with private deeds, not public words."

Despite Bogart's hatred of sentiment, Betty revealed two occasions when he cried. The first time was in New York before they were married. He had gone two weeks ahead and when she arrived there was a big powwow with the press and she was delayed in meeting him. When Betty telephoned to explain the delay, Bogart was furious. "You actresses are all alike," he scolded. "Your career comes above everything else."

Betty left the party and went to Bogart's suite. When she walked in the door he started to cry. "He didn't think I would come," she said.

Afer their wedding ceremony, Betty saw him cry again when he first saw Stephen in his schoolroom. "I think the impact of fatherhood caught up with him," she said.

The fact is it was the birth of Stephen, and later Leslie, that seemed more than anything else to bring Bogart to the realization that he was married. "After the children were born you could see him become mellower," said Mary Baker.

Bogart had never wanted children in his first three marriages. Then, when he married Betty, he felt he was too old. He also believed that a husband and wife are one unit until there is a child. He was afraid that when Betty became a mother she would be preoccupied with the child and have too little time for him. Underneath his occasional rudeness toward his wife he had a very real, if puzzling, dependence upon her.

Betty told me of the night she announced to Bogie, who was then forty-nine years old, that they were going to have a baby, their first. "He had just come from the studio and I met him outside the house," she said. "He knew I had gone to the doctor's to see if I was pregnant, and when he saw me coming toward him he asked casually, 'What's new, Betty?'

"I told him quietly that we were going to have a baby.

"He didn't jump up and down or even act excited. He just got kind of quiet and emotional and put an arm around me as we walked into the house. Nothing else was said about the baby all through dinner and the rest of the evening.

"That night we had one of our biggest arguments. I don't remember what it was about now, and not once did the word 'baby' ever get mentioned, but I knew that was what had brought the argument on. Bogie was just expressing his resentment that he—like most other married men—was about to become a father."

When the news that the Bogarts were about to become parents reached the Romanoff crowd, there was unrestrained glee. One of the women suggested a baby shower for Betty. "I wouldn't give one for Betty, but I would give one for Bogie," said Harry Kurnitz. The idea met with instant acclaim and the shower was arranged on a stag basis at the upstairs room at Romanoff's.

After dinner everybody took turns toasting Bogie. Mike Romanoff got up and in his cultured Guardsman voice started out by saying he wanted to pay tribute to his dear friend who was not like the other chicken pluckers in town. He then went into a thirty-minute discussion of Howard Hughes, eventually shifted to comments on Linda Darnell, and never mentioned Bogart again.

The other speeches were equally irrelevant to the occasion. By 9 P.M. Collier Young and John Huston had Bogart on the floor while Huston delivered the "baby" with fireplace tongs.

Then Bogart sat on a couch and received the gifts: layettes, silver mugs, and other baby presents. "By the third gift Bogie was so choked up about the fact that he was going to have a genuine baby that he was in tears," recalled Kurnitz. "He made a speech but he was too confused with emotion and booze to make sense. He wanted to make it a square speech, but it wasn't in him to do it."

On the day that Stephen was born, Bogart went to work at the studio. Betty timed the pains herself in the morning, called the doctor, and drove herself to his office. After the examination, he called Bogie, who rushed to the doctor's office looking absolutely green. He drove Betty to Cedars of Lebanon Hospital and went into the labor room with her. "He stayed as long as he could take it," Betty said. "But his face got whiter and whiter and, finally, he said he would have to leave."

Jaik Rosenstein, who had left Warner's to work for Hedda Hopper, went to the hospital to keep Bogart company. "When

I got off the elevator on the fourth floor I saw Bogie in the waiting room white as as sheet," said Rosenstein. " 'You goddam ghoul, what are you doing here?' he asked me.

" 'You shouldn't talk to a member of the fourth estate that way,' kidded the obstetrician, Dr. Prinzmetal.

" 'He's no member of the fourth estate, he's a friend of mine,' said Bogie. 'Come on in and have a drink.' "

Although Bogart could stand pain himself, he couldn't bear to think of his wife or children undergoing it. When Stephen was three the doctor came to examine him for a hernia. He had to probe to see whether an operation would be needed, and he had Betty holding the boy's hands and Bogie his feet. Bogie winced with every probe, got pale, and said, "Better hurry, doctor, or I'll have to leave."

"He nearly passed out," recalled Betty, who said that Bogie never mentioned the incident to her again, but the next day she heard him on the telephone telling Nunnally Johnson that he should have seen Stephen, braver than a soldier. "His voice rang with a pride that I had never imagined Bogie would feel. That night he went in while Steve was sleeping in his crib and looked at him for a long time saying nothing. Later, when the question of having another child came up, Bogie said he wanted one if I could guarantee another like Stephen."

When Bogie was fifty-four Betty gave birth to a daughter, who was christened Leslie Howard after Bogart's friend and mentor. The birth of a daughter was something very special to Bogie, as it is to most men. He was afraid of her at first, but gradually he realized that though she was a female she was also his.

"I've finally begun to understand why men carry pictures of their children with them," he told me once at Romanoff's, adding needlessly, "They're proud of them."

When Ed Murrow and his television crew came to the Bogart house to do a "Person to Person" show, Betty and Bogie were frightened that Stephen would look into the cameras and say to Murrow, "Hello Blubber Head."

"He calls everyone Blubber Head," Bogie told me. "Worse, he might use one of his other pet names like Mr. Dog-Do-in-the-Pants."

Their worries were groundless, although the show was memorable for Leslie. It was the first time she had seen her father wearing his toupee, which at first she thought was a hair hat.

Richard Gehman wrote that life around the house with Bogie was a good example of the way that nature sometimes imitated art. Some of the things that went on with Bogart *père* might have been copied directly from a Humphrey Bogart-Lauren Bacall movie.

One summer afternoon as Gehman and Bogart were sitting down in Bogart's paneled den for a drink and a talk, a series of startling sounds came from the kitchen at the opposite end of the house. First there was a loud scream, then a slap, followed by derisive laughter. Bogie tensed in his chair and leaned forward. Another scream followed the first, then more laughter.

"Excuse me," Bogart said, "I got to go and belt somebody."

He stalked toward the kitchen, looking exactly like a Humphrey Bogart film character heading into the villain's hideout to clean things up.

Gehman could hear Bogie say in that menacing voice of his, "What's going on in here, anyhow?"

"Steve," said Leslie in a whimpering little four-year-old voice, "was shooting me with rubber bands."

"Is that true?" Bogie demanded.

"Aw," said Steve, aged seven, "I wasn't shooting her much."

"You were, too," Leslie charged indignantly.

"I was not!"

"Wait a minute," Bogie said. "Steve, you shut up. I don't want to have to rap you. Listen, you got no right shooting your sister with rubber bands. She's littler than you, and besides she's female. They cause us a lot of trouble, but we got to endure it. They're not as strong as we are."

"She was teasing me and she was teasing Jim [a white mouse]," said Steve.

"I don't care what she was doing to you or Jim," Bogie said. "You're in the wrong. Come on, now. Be a good boy. Be a gentleman. It sounds like a rat fight in here."

Bogie came back to the den, and sat down, his scarred mouth grim but not enough to conceal his amusement at the scene he had just played with his children.

While Lauren Bacall was making *Blood Alley* in San Francisco, Bogart called me to ask if I wanted to spend the weekend with him and Betty on location. "We'll go up on the evening train to see Betty, and then maybe on Saturday we can go to the zoo," he said, rather more quietly than usual.

"Who's going to the zoo?" I asked.

"We are—you, me, Stephen and Betty," he said.

"You want me along as baby sitter for Stephen?" I asked.

"Hell, no," said Bogie. "I want you along for company." He paused, then admitted, "You've got kids. I figure maybe youll know what to do when Steve acts up."

Before meeting Bogie and Steve at the train I took the precaution of stopping at a five-and-dime and buying some crayons, coloring books, and little toys that I thought might amuse a six-year-old boy.

Bogart was waiting at the gate for me, standing hand-in-hand with his son, neat as an Eton scholar. There was a worried frown on Bogie's face. "First time I've been alone with the kid this long," he said. "I hope it works out all right."

Noticing the paper bag I was carrying he asked me what was in it. I told him.

"You're a genius, kid, and I knew it," he said.

It was 8:30 before the train got started and we found our compartment. Bogart was for "bedding down the kid" and going in to the dining car for some liquid refreshment and a snack. But Steve, who was lolling comfortably in an upper bunk, insisted on a fairy tale. "I don't know any fairy tales," said Bogart. "Uncle Joe will tell you one."

"No," said Steve firmly. "I want you to tell it to me. Mother always tells me a fairy tale before I go to sleep."

Bogart looked at me for a suggestion. "Spin it out," I said, kicking off my shoes and climbing into a lower berth on the other side of the compartment. Bogart took off his shoes, too, and climbed in next to me. "You tell me what to say and I'll repeat it," he said. So I started to improvise a story about a six-year-old boy on a train trip, with Bogart echoing the words after me. Twenty minues later Steve was asleep. So was his father.

In the morning when the porter knocked on the door Bogie walked over to Steve, who was still sleeping soundly, and kissed him tenderly on the forehead. Then he backed off and gave him a quizzical searching stare accompanied by a tugging of the ear—Bogart's signal that he was thinking deeply. In a gruff voice, he woke Steve up. Later on the trip I caught Bogie giving Steve the same quizzical look again. "I don't know," he told me. "I guess maybe I had the kid too late in life. I just don't know what to do about him." Then, kind of shamefacedly, he said, "But I love him. I hope he knows that."

When he was not working and the children were away at

school Bogart was bored. "He simply didn't know what to do with himself," Betty said. "Unfortunately, I got him at a bad time. He had already gone through the golf stage and other pastimes that men acquire, then give up. He had discarded them all and was left with nothing.

"So he would spend two or three hours at lunch in Romanoff's every day gabbing with his cronies. Then he would come home and take a nap which consumed another hour. By that time it was the hour to have a drink and get ready for dinner."

When he was working and things went wrong, Bogart was like most husbands: He would take it out on his wife. If everything was fine Betty knew it the minute he came in the door. On occasions when they were going to have company and it was important that he be in a good humor, Betty would try and pick a day when he didn't work. Then she stayed out of his way as much as possible. That way, he had a fair chance of reaching the evening with unruffled temperament and without needling.

"He was never averse to sharpening his wits on my ego," said Betty, good-naturedly. "His needling was a process of using words which stick you where you are most vulnerable and where you least expect it. I watched Bogie needle many people in my time, and I had the treatment so often I'm sure my psyche looks like a dope addict's arm, because Bogie knew my weak spots.

"For example, every time I went to work I felt guilty about leaving the kids. I worried about what would happen when I was away, and I thought deep down that maybe I was being cruel by leaving them. If Bogie was in a needling mood or if he didn't want me to leave at that time he'd start off by making cracks about my being a 'career woman.'

" 'You giving up your children for your career?' he would ask.

" 'Who do you think you are, another Duse or Bernhardt [those were the only actresses in Bogart's book]? Your career comes before our kids, eh? Just like every other actress.'

"If I already felt guilty about going to work I usually let him leave the field a victor. On occasion I snapped back, saying that we could use the money I made. He dismissed this by claiming my money only put us in another tax bracket and it really cost us money."

Like most women, Betty prided herself on being a good

wife. She selected all of her husband's clothes, took care of the children, and ran their home to the best of her ability. As in ordinary households, however, there were times when things seemed to get ahead of her.

Bogart never missed the chance to come in with a sock in his hand, pointing dramatically to a hole. "You've got time to go out and be an actress but no time to darn my socks," he'd say, then storm out of the room.

To people who didn't know him well, Bogie's needling was, to say the least, disconcerting. They didn't understand that to him needling was an activity of the mind and spirit. He wanted to get a reaction from them in the hope of stirring up a little excitement. No one was immune to his shafts, not his wife or his friends; not even the press.

SIX

The first time I met Bogie he asked me what I wanted to drink.

"A Coke, please," I said.

"You don't drink?" Bogart asked, adding hopefully, "You A.A.?"

"Nope," I said. "I never drank."

Bogart, who was behind the bar in his den, accepted this news without comment for a moment. But when he stepped out with a glass of Scotch in his hand he said, "I don't trust any bastard who doesn't drink—especially a pipe-smoking newspaperman. You must have something to hide. People who don't drink are afraid of revealing themselves.

"Furthermore," he said, "I don't trust any man who has more hair than I have."

Having delivered himself of a pronouncement I was to hear many times in the coming years, he turned again to the bar. I picked up my pad and pencil and started for the door.

"Where are you going?" Bogart asked.

"How are we going to do an interview if we start out with your not trusting me?" I asked. "I don't drink and I certainly have more hair on my head than you do, but then so do most men."

Bogart thought that over for a moment. "You're just going to have to work that much harder to make me trust you," he said. Shooing a couple of boxer dogs off a seat, he gestured for me to sit down.

That was our introduction, and the routine of insult followed by wary acceptance became our standard every time

104

I saw him over the next decade. He finally trusted me, but it took a long time. Even then, when I went to visit him at his home where he was dying, he called me a "freeloader like all the rest of the press."

But that was Bogart and, as the late Peter Lorre once said, "I like Bogie because he is one hundred percent what he is and that is very rich if you know him. So you take all the disadvantages with the advantages."

For me, at least, the advantages always outweighed the disadvantages. When I first came to Hollywood as a columnist for the New York *Herald Tribune* I had very few contacts, knew very few stars, had seen very few pictures, and was not in any sense a film fan. On interviews I tended to ask naïvely fresh and frequently impertinent questions, which soon earned me a reputation as a needler.

Bogie liked me, probably because I stood up to him on our first interview and because as a sociologist and ex-teacher I viewed my life in Hollywood as life among the savages. He took me in hand, functioning more as an old newspaper reporter than as an actor. I soon learned that he was well equipped to be an editor. He was surprisingly well read, and not merely in the best sellers but in the classics as well. Bogie had a good knowledge of American history and Greek mythology.

He could and did quote from Plato, Emerson, Pope, and many English dramatists. (He could quote more than a thousand lines from Shakespeare.) Once we had a long discussion about Anthony Trollope's works.

His contacts around the world were extraordinary; he corresponded regularly with Harold Laski and Justice Holmes. He subscribed to the *Harvard Law Review* and his range of interests was remarkable. In addition, human behavior no longer startled or surprised him, no matter what nonsensical form it happened to take. He was rarely bored except by boors.

He would read my columns and call me on the telephone to criticize them kindly but candidly. In those days, I tried to do word portraits of my interview subjects in 750 words covering a variety of subjects and paraphrasing quotes or trimming them down and cleaning up grammatical errors.

One day Bogie suggested I interview my next star on just one subject and quote him at length precisely, grammatical errors and all. I did as suggested. The technique worked remarkably well.

"I told you it would work," said Bogie, delighted with the result.

Occasionally, he would suggest that I interview someone like Frank Sinatra or Spencer Tracy. When I would protest that it was not easy to arrange such an interview he would say, "Let me handle it." Minutes later he would call back to say that Sinatra was expecting me.

Thanks to Bogie's sponsorship and friendship many of the stars most Hollywood reporters could not contact soon became available to me. Most stars are columnist-shy, but they felt that if Bogie trusted me, I could be trusted. And although some of my columns tended to make fools of the stars, I quoted them precisely, which soon earned me a reputation for being a fair reporter.

Many times I would talk over a column with Bogie before writing it. Sometimes I used him as a sounding board on stories. His criticism was always pertinent. He was not averse, however, to using me to stir up a little trouble when the mood was on him and he saw some fun in it for himself and profit for me. Burt Lancaster still doesn't speak to me because of a column Bogart inspired.

I had done an interview with Lancaster at Columbia Studios in which he said that he was going to do *Judgment at Nuremburg,* because it was a picture in which he could become emotionally involved and which should be made. He said he wanted to do it even though he would get paid very little money and had only one good scene opposite Spencer Tracy, whom he admired.

As the devil wanted it, I dropped by to see Bogart, who was working on another stage. As part of our routine greeting, I needled him by saying that he ought to be like Lancaster, willing to do a picture because it should be done even though the part, billing, and pay were small.

Bogart shrugged. "Why don't you read Lancaster's quotes to Spence," he said. "You might get an interesting response."

I found Tracy on another set and read Lancaster's quotes to him. It turned out that Lancaster was going to be paid half a million dollars for the role. His one scene with Tracy was seven pages long, during which Tracy didn't say a word. In addition, he was going to get star billing with Tracy.

I wrote the column, quoting both men. Bogart called the day after it appeared to congratulate me—and warn that Lancaster was looking around town for me so he could knock my head off. Bogart was delighted.

As Nunnally Johnson once said, "Bogie thought of himself as Scaramouche, the mischievous scamp who sets off the fireworks, then nips out."

To Bogie, needling was an exercise of the mind as well as of the spirit. And if practice makes perfect, he was expert at it. Most of his friends agree that his pattern of insulting and needling both friends and foes began when he arrived in Hollywood, because he felt Hollywood people were, for the most part, pompous phonies. "Bigwigs have been known to stay away from the brilliant Hollywood occasions rather than expose their swelling neck muscles to Bogart's banderillas," said John Huston.

"Bogie could be pretty exasperating at times," Nunnally Johnson said. "He never stopped thinking how he could stir things up a little. I don't think it was an act—it was natural in Bogie. He was an ingrained mischief maker."

In Johnson's opinion, Bogie demonstrated social brinkmanship on its highest level. "He had dozens of ingenious ways of avoiding disaster," Johnson said. "It really was an art. His psychological timing was perfect."

One day when Johnson was with Bogie and Betty she gave him a fierce bawling out for his behavior at a party the previous night. He had needled Rock Hudson about his first name, suggesting that a new star would come along named Dung Heap and knock Rock on his Butt End— ". . . and there's another name you might adopt."

"Who the hell do you think you are, Bogart?" Betty said. "You might have had your neck broken."

"Easy, easy, old girl," he said soothingly. "I wish you would realize that there is a real art in getting this close to calamity."

Certainly Bogie knew when his needling would precipitate violence, and he almost always pulled up just short of it. But if things got rough, he had ways of handling that, too. "I have two rules for fighting," he once told me over lunch at Romanoff's. "First, any time a guy wants to start a fight in a club be sure there's a big headwaiter around. Hit the guy first, then get near the waiter, who will stop the fight.

"Second, and equally important: Never step outside."

Harry Kurnitz, who was present at many of Bogart's near brawls, agreed that he followed his rules closely. "Bogie's animosity and arrogance ranged in direct ratio to the number of people holding him back," Kurnitz said. "The truth is, I believe, that Bogie lived his whole life without ever having been in a fight."

Bogie always seemed able to avoid a real, knockdown fight and often referred to himself as a physical coward—which he wasn't—and once told me he hated the sight of blood. "My father was a doctor and I saw too much of it when I was a child," he explained.

A typical Bogart brawl, illustrating both his debating style and his sense of self-preservation, occurred one night at a party at Louis Calhern's house. Bogie overheard an argument director Norman Panama was having with agent Paul Small—who was not aptly named: He was big.

Panama was saying that he thought Danny Kaye was the greatest talent in show business. Small said he wasn't, that Lenny Kent was the greatest.

At this point Bogart entered the conversation. "What would you know about it, you tub of lard?" he asked Small.

The agent angrily grabbed Bogart's wrist.

Bogart looked around the room and saw that his host was coming to the rescue. He snarled, "Let go of that wrist or I'll let you have this glass in the face."

Small held on. Just as Calhern, a big man, reached the group, Bogart heaved the glass full of liquor at Small, who ducked. The liquor splashed on Mrs. Small, Dore Schary's sister. Betty screamed. Calhern separated the combatants. Once again Bogie had looked tough, as fearless as any screen hero—and gotten away with it.

Another time Bogart figured a great excuse for following his rule number two. At a party at Milton Bren and Claire Trevor's house he was almost falling-down drunk and was enlivening things by needling the host and other guests with too much vulgarity to suit Bren, who finally said, "Cut it out, Bogie."

Bogie kept it up. "I'm damn sick of your vulgarity," Milton said. "Step outside with me—I'm going to knock hell out of you."

"Sure, I will," said Bogart. "Just help me up, please." Everybody broke up—Bogart's superb brinkmanship had won the day as it did on the afternoon Sid Luft and Judy Garland came to his house to pour out their family troubles.

Richard Burton recalled the afternoon. "Bogie told Sid and Judy to get out, stay out, and never come back, that he was fed up with their problems. He added a few choice epithets and ended by admonishing Sid 'to take that dull wife of yours with you.' "

"I've a good mind to bust your face in," growled Luft, a husky man who had once been a test pilot.

Bogart backed off a few steps, grinned, and said, "Sid, you won't lay a hand on me."

Nonplussed, Luft stopped a haymaker in midair to ask, "Why not?"

"Because, Sid, you're my friend," Bogart said gently. ("It was a magnificent moment," Burton reported.)

Arms around each other, Bogart and Luft strolled over to his bar, raised glasses, and the incident was closed.

While it is undoubtedly true that Bogie generally evaded combat himself while inciting disputes between others, on several occasions he risked destruction by trying to hold up his end as a tough guy. At a formal New Year's Eve party given by director Lewis Milestone, Bogie was introduced to Jeff Cassell, a Hollywood writer who had been with the Free French underground during World War II.

"I hear you're a tough guy," said Cassell.

"No, I'm not tough," said Bogart. "I just seem tough."

"Do something tough," challenged Cassell.

"You got the wrong guy," said Bogart.

"I can eat glass," said Cassell, who chewed up and swallowed a champagne glass. Bogart expressed the admiration of a Penrod watching Huck Finn.

"I can also eat razor blades," said Cassell, who borrowed one from the host and proceeded to swallow it. Again Bogart applauded but declined to try the trick.

"Well," urged Cassell, "if you can't do that, let's mix some drinks."

He mixed some vermouth, Scotch, bourbon, brandy, champagne, and gin in a glass. Downing half, he gave the rest to Bogart, who now was on familiar ground. When Bogart finished the glass, Cassell nodded approval but said, "I still don't think you're tough. You can't eat the glass."

"I can so," said Bogart, who rapped his glass on the bar to shatter it, then put a piece in his mouth, chewed it, and tried to swallow. Nothing went down, but blood gushed copiously from his cut mouth.

"I guess you are all right," said Cassell. "We are both very tough guys. Let us go now and insult the women together."

Although Swifty Lazar believes that Bogart hurt many

people with his needling, the idea of the game was to pick on someone who was able to take care of himself. Lazar recalled the night that Bogart needled Hollywood attorney Greg Bautzer so much that finally Bautzer asked him to step outside.

"I'm going to beat you to a pulp," Bautzer threatened.

"You're not going to hit an old man, are you?" asked Bogart.

"Well, stop needling me," said Bautzer.

"You have a bad pattern to your life, Greg," said Bogart sadly.

"That does it," yelled Bautzer, who got to his feet and invited Bogart to step outside.

"Go on," said Bogart. "You go first. Everyone will follow us if we both go out together. Let's fight in private."

Bautzer marched outside. Bogart finished his drink and had another. Five minutes later Bautzer came back in the room looking for him.

"You look cold to me," said Bogart. "Come on, let's have a drink."

Again brinkmanship saved the day.

Bogart's needling, however, was frequently on the level of practical joking with a favorite victim—his good friend, Mike Romanoff. The restaurateur intensely disliked Preston Sturges, the movie director and writer. One day Bogie was out drinking with Bob Coote, an English actor, who was staying with Romanoff. Bogie and Coote picked up Sturges, got him completely drunk, and then deposited him in Romanoff's living room to the host's horror.

Romanoff demanded that all guests at his establishment wear ties. One day when Bogart arrived without a tie Romanoff insisted he cover his neck with a napkin. The next day Bogart arrived with a tie no more than one-half inch long at his neck. "It was so small it was hardly visible," said Romanoff, "but what could I do?"

Director Richard Brooks told me of the time Romanoff and Bogart agreed to play twenty games of chess with the proviso that if Bogart won two games of the twenty Romanoff would give $100 to charity. If Bogie didn't win two, he would give the money to charity. Out of the first three games, Bogie won two. Before the next game could be played off, Romanoff had to go to the hospital for a minor operation. Rather than interrupt the match, Romanoff agreed that he would telephone his moves to Bogart, who would be in his usual booth at Romanoff's.

Romanoff still insisted he was the better player, so he challenged Bogie and Brooks to play against him. Bogie arranged for two telephones to be in his booth. When Romanoff telephoned his moves Bogie said, "Wait a moment while Dick and I consult." Then he telephoned Max Steiner, U.S. chess champion, who was in on the gag. Steiner suggested the countermoves. When Romanoff sent the check to charity, Bogie told him with great glee of the stunt.

Another of Bogie's frequent targets was the agent, Swifty Lazar, who on at least one occasion topped him. The incident happened one New Year's weekend at Frank Sinatra's home in Palm Springs. Bogie plotted to push Swifty into the swimming pool. Swifty is a rare dandy, and Bogie knew he would be upset to have his clothes ruined.

Finally, he saw his chance and gleefully shoved Swifty into the water. Swifty changed into dry clothes and waited for his turn. When Bogart was not looking Swifty shoved him into the pool. Bogart was furious because he was wearing a thousand-dollar Audemars Piguet watch Betty had just given him for Christmas.

When he dried out in front of the fireplace, Bogart tossed the watch to Swifty and asked, "What are you going to do about this?"

"I'm going to dry it out, Bogie," said Swifty, and threw the timepiece into the fireplace.

Bogart didn't cool down until the next day when Swifty presented him with an elaborately wrapped box. Bogie beamed. He unwrapped the box and found another, equally elaborate. Still beaming, he unwrapped three more boxes-within-boxes, until he got to the last one. Happily opening it he found a two-dollar Mickey Mouse watch handsomely engraved: "With great admiration." Months later Swifty gave him a new Audemars Piguet.

Bogart in public was little different from Bogart in private except that, frequently, he was the target thanks to his public image. For years whenever he went into nightclubs, some stranger would strut over to his table to pinch his muscles and sneer, "So you think you're tough?" Bogart called these hecklers "creeps" and nothing distressed him more than to be accosted by one who wanted to slug it out with him for the pleasure of boasting that he had bested Bogart, the killer.

His usual answer to the stock question—"So you think you're tough?"—was a tired smile and soft answer. But sometimes his patience would be worn thin and he would react in the way expected of him.

One night at El Morocco in New York when a man teased, "All right, Louey, drop the gun" (a line he never said in any film), Bogart's lips tightened in the classic manner of Duke Mantee. He reached out with his lighted cigarette and jabbed at the stranger's face. As a result Bogart was asked to leave and not return.

But like the traditional criminal Bogart had a penchant for visiting the scene of the crime. Less than six months later he was back in El Morocco shortly before 3 o'clock on a Sunday morning with a pal. Both men were carrying stuffed pandas that Bogart had bought for his son, Steve.

Noticing a friend across the room, the men put the stuffed animals on a table and went over for a drink. They returned a few minutes later in time to surprise two girls in the act of making off with the pandas. Bogart tackled one of the young ladies. In the ensuing scuffle a flying plate hit the other one on the hip.

It could have been an expensive evening as the girl later brought a suit for $25,000 damages. Bogart refused to take the suit seriously, though. When he was asked in court, "Were you drunk at that time?" he cracked back, "Isn't everybody at three in the morning?"

Sometimes, in public, Bogie would retreat into his screen image because it was expected of him—and because it was fun. Nathaniel Benchley witnessed such a show.

"The first time I saw him I was with someone who knew him well and decided to put on a little show for the benefit of the people who were enjoying their dinners. He went out to the bar and tapped Bogart on the shoulder.

" 'All right,' he said, 'finish your drink and get out of here. We don't want you in this place.'

"Bogart looked around, slowly and ominously took his cigarette out of his mouth and flipped it to the ground, and moved up so that their faces were eight inches apart. He squinted as he spat out the last of his cigarette smoke. A waiter looked nervously at the bartender, who reached one hand under the counter.

" 'Listen,' snarled Bogart. 'I'm staying here, and if you don't like it you can move along. This is my territory and you know it. Or do I have to prove it to you?'

United Press International Newspictures

25. Humphrey with Sally Rand in *Rain*.

26. *Hell's Bells,* with Shirley Booth, opened January 26, 1925, and played fifteen weeks.

Culver Pictures, Inc.

27. Humphrey and Mary Boland in *Cradle Snatchers*, a 1925 comedy that ran forty-two weeks.

Culver Pictures, Inc.

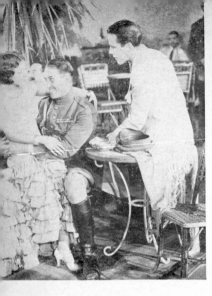

28. Bogie played a rich youngster in *A Devil with Women* starring Victor McLaglen and Mona Maris, released November, 1930, by Fox.

29. *After All* with Helen Haye and Margaret Perry opened at the Booth Theatre on December 3, 1931.

30. *I Loved You Wednesday*, a 1932 play with Rose Hobart.

Culver Pictures, Inc.

31. On January 7, 1935, Humphrey opened as Duke Mantee in the Broadway production of *The Petrified Forest* starring Leslie Howard.

United Press International Newspictures

Culver Pictures, Inc.

32. H u m p h r e y with
Claire Luce in *Up the
River,* his second movie,
released by Fox in Octo-
ber, 1930.

Culver Pictures, Inc.

33. Warner Brothers released *The
Petrified Forest* in February, 1936, and
Humphrey's Duke Mantee became a
blueprint for every cinematic gangster
of the era.

34. In *Big City Blues,* September, 1932, Warner Brothers, Humphrey got tenth billing.

Culver Pictures, Inc.

35. Humphrey with Barton Mac-Lane and Edward G. Robinson in *Bullets or Ballots,* released in June, 1936, by Warner Brothers.

36. Racketeers masquerade as patriots under black hoods in *Black Legion,* released by Warner Brothers in January, 1937.

37. Bogie played Joe "Red" Kennedy in *San Quentin,* released by Warner Brothers in August, 1937.

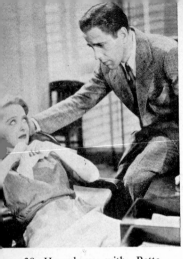

Culver Pictures, Inc.

38. Humphrey with Bette Davis in *Marked Woman* released in April, 1937, by Warner Brothrs.

39. Bogie with Edward G. Robinson in *The Amazing Dr. Clitterhouse* released by Warner's in July, 1938.

40. *King of the Underworld* with Kay Francis was released by Warner's in January, 1939.

41. James Cagney and Humphrey in *Oklahoma Kid,* which was released by Warner Brothers in March, 1939.

42. Humphrey with Bette Davis in *Dark Victory,* released by W a r n e r Brothers in April, 1939.

43. *The Roaring Twenties* was released in October, 1939, by Warner Brothers.

44. Humphrey in *The Return of Dr. X*, released by Warner Brothers in December, 1939.

45. Humphrey as John Murrell in *Virginia City*, released by Warner's in March, 1940.

46. Humphrey, George Raft, and Ann Sheridan in *They Drive by Night*, released by Warner Brothers in August, 1940.

47. Humphrey plays Sam Spade, with Peter L o r r e, in Dashiell Hammett's *The Maltese Falcon,* released by Warner Brothers in October, 1941.

48. Humphrey took the role of Roy Earle with Ida Lupino in *High Sierra,* released in January, 1941, by Warner Brothers.

49. Humphrey as Rick with Ingrid Bergman and Dooley Wilson in *Casablanca,* released in January, 1943, by Warner Brothers. Humphrey had just signed a seven-year contract for $3,500 a week, forty weeks a year, no option.

50. Patrick O'Moore, Bogie, and Carl Harbord on location during *Sahara*, 1943.

Patrick O'Moore

51. Patrick O'Moore, Mayo Methot (Mrs. B.), and Bogie taking a lunch break during *Conflict* in 1944. The film was released in June, 1945.

Patrick O'Moore

52. *To Have and Have Not*, Betty's first picture, made when she was nineteen and Humphrey forty-five. The film, based on the novel by Ernest Hemingway, was released in January, 1945.

53. Bogie and Betty appeared together in *The Big Sleep* by Raymond Chandler, released by Warner Brothers in August, 1946.

54. Humphrey and Lizabeth Scott in *Dead Reckoning,* released by Columbia in February, 1947.

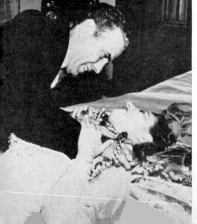

55. The strangling of Barbara Stanwyck in *The Two Mrs. Carrolls,* released by Warner Brothers in May, 1947.

56. In 1947, "B and B" did *Dark Passage* together for Warner Brothers.

57. John Huston directed Humphrey, Walter Huston, Bruce Bennett, and Tim Holt in *The Treasure of the Sierra Madre,* released in January, 1948, by Warner's.

58. Bogie played a hero returning to his Tokyo nightclub in *Tokyo Joe,* a Santana Production released by Columbia in November, 1949.

59. Humphrey tries to choke Gloria Grahame during *In a Lonely Place,* a Santana Production released by Columbia in August, 1950.

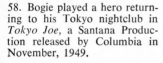

60. Betty and Bogie appeared again in *Key Largo,* released by Warner's in July, 1948, directed by John Huston and with Edward G. Robinson, Lionel Barrymore, and Claire Trevor.

61. John Huston directed Humphrey and Katharine Hepburn in *The African Queen*, for which Bogie won an Oscar for Best Actor of 1951.

62. In *Sirocco*, a Santana Production released by Columbia in July, 1951, Bogie played an expatriate American gun smuggler.

63. Bogie and Robert Middleton in *The Desperate Hours,* directed by William Wyler and released by Paramount in November, 1955.

64. Truman Capote wrote the script for *Beat the Devil,* starring Bogie with Jennifer Jones, Gina Lollobrigida, and Peter Lorre, released in March, 1954.

65. Humphrey with Van Johnson and José Ferrer in *The Caine Mutiny,* which was based on the novel by Herman Wouk.

66. Twentieth Century-Fox released *The Left Hand of God* in September, 1955.

Culver Pictures, Inc.

67. Humphrey Bogart's last film was *The Harder They Fall*, from Budd Schulberg's novel, released by Columbia in April, 1956.

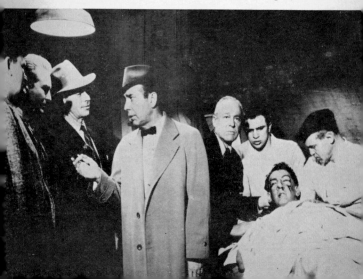

"The nearest person at the bar slid back a couple of yards, his eyes popping, and a few of the other guests began nervously to get themselves behind the furniture.

"The whole thing blew over when Bogart broke down and began to laugh. But I learned later that the two had on occasion come to blows—pulling their punches, but pretending that they were cutting each other to ribbons."

Clifton Webb was a frequent partner to this routine. The elegant actor, who was of the opinion that Bogart was a "warm, friendly fellow," said, "He and I had a running gag. We insulted each other at every party. It was just an act but he loved to see people's eyebrows go up."

Despite all his tough talk, in his candid moments, Bogart never pretended to any vast stock of courage. But Peter Viertel, the screenwriter, remembered vividly the time when he saw Bogart meet his own test: He revealed the truth about himself under pressure.

The incident took place in Stanleyville, Africa, while Bogart was filming *The African Queen* with Katharine Hepburn. "Kate was crazy about African art," Viertel said. "Bogie, Betty, and I hired a boat to go up the river to have a look at some art in a village. As we cast off from the dock the guide went below to start the engine. When it didn't catch, he lit a match. The fumes inside the hold exploded. The man leaped into the water and threw himself on the sand in agony. Meanwhile, the burning boat started to float down the river toward a river steamer.

"Bogie acted like a trained fireman. 'Pete, there's a fire extinguisher on the forward bulkhead, get it.' I did, but it was empty. Bogie meanwhile managed to steer us near enough to the steamer to throw them a line. We unloaded the women, then he stayed aboard to help put out the fire. In the moment of truth, he had guts like Manolete."

SEVEN

Bogart was the King of Hollywood in the fifties. Like King Arthur, he had a Round Table and a retinue of knights (later famous as the Clan or the Rat Pack). The castle where they foregathered every midday belonged to Prince Michael Romanoff, proprietor of a restaurant he named after himself in Beverly Hills. Mike was one of the most colorful figures in Hollywood. He is neither a prince, nor is his real name Mike. His antecedents are vague and certainly not royal, and it is hard to believe today that in bygone years he made a career of posing as His Imperial Highness, the Prince Michael Alexandrovitch Dmitri Obolensky Romanoff, nephew of the last of the Czars. Phony prince or not, Mike was beloved by the ultrasnobbish film crowd, which actually accepted him as its social arbiter.

"I like Romanoff's because it's the only place to go," Bogart told reporter Ezra Goodman. "I like Mike very, very much. He is a very entertaining, interesting, and kind man, a civilized citizen. I can meet my friends here. It's kind of like a club."

When he was not working Bogart invariably arrived at Romanoff's at 12:30 P.M. and always occupied the second booth from the left off the entryway. Soon that booth became the Number One table in the restaurant. Bogart's lunch usually consisted of two martinis, and either bacon and eggs, a lamb chop or hamburger with a beer or milk. Coffee was followed by Drambuie. "Bogie didn't really enjoy food—he only ate to stay alive," Mike Romanoff told me.

Waiters in red jackets busied themselves around tables

crowded with some of the best-known faces in the world. It was at Romanoff's that much of the action and fun in Bogart's life took place. A gag of which he never tired was to sit in his booth and con someone else into picking up his lunch check. He had developed all manner of devices to stiff other people. This was not meanness or avarice on Bogart's part—it was a game.

But life was a game for him and Hollywood was different then. Romanoff's is gone and now in the Oak Bar of the Beverly Wilshire Hotel, a block away, one hears only talk of "thous" and "mils," "capital gains" and "spreads." Laughter and drunkenness is frowned on in such an atmosphere, but Romanoff's in the old days was a place for fun and games, not wheeling and dealing. Today the lunch check is sought after, not avoided, as year-end proof of a business expense.

From many interviews there, marinated with nostalgia, and with the help of screenwriter Peter Viertel's ear for dialogue, I will reconstruct one of those Romanoff luncheon sessions.

At 12:30 the Bogarts arrive at the entrance to the main dining room, three steps lower than the bar entrance. Descent from the bar to the main hall is by invitation only. Seating is a delicate social ritual performed by the Prince or Reinhardt, the headwaiter.

The dining room is crowded with famous folk in various stages of tanning. It is a Hollywood axiom that, excepting Cary Grant, an actor with a deep, dark tan is living at the beach "at liberty"; sunburned actors are newly arrived from New York; and evenly tanned, not too dark actors like the Bogarts have acquired their color by a swimming pool.

Bogart is well dressed in gray flannels and a black cashmere jacket with a neat checked bow tie. Mrs. Bogart is wearing the latest in elegant Paris fashion.

The arrival of the Bogarts causes a stir among the tourists who were chosen discriminately and placed by the management against the far wall where they can see but not be heard. The regulars, Jack Benny, Peter Lawford, Frank Sinatra, Gary Cooper, and MCA agents George Chasin and Herman Citron, acknowledge the Bogarts' arrival with smiles and waves but continue with their eating. The stage is set and the audience is in their seats, which Bogart notes with a glance around the room.

After brief pleasantries with Reinhardt, the Bogarts are seated. Romanoff, who has been talking with film producer

Collier Young, comes to greet them. He moves as he speaks —slowly and carefully. He is a small man with an incongruous "butch" haircut that gives his genial face a military look. His clothes are frantically dapper—a very English blazer, flannels, and bench-made shoes.

"Hello, my darling Betty," Romanoff says in a faultless, carefully cultivated Oxford accent as he kisses her proffered cheeks, one after the other. "I see you're still with the same aging actor."

"I can't live without him," says Mrs. Bogart.

"Good morning, your royal phoniness," says Bogart with obvious affection.

"It may be morning to you, but it's afternoon to working people," says Romanoff, who starts to move off.

"Join us in a drink, Mike?" asks Bogart.

Romanoff, who will not sit down unless invited, settles next to Bogart. "I should be most honored to do so," he says, in the formal manner he affects.

"Swifty is paying, of course," says Bogart. Romanoff nods happily. According to the rules of the game, the gauntlet had been flung. Swifty Lazar, the literary agent, had been elected to pay the lunch check that day, though he was as yet unaware that the vote had been polled and he had won.

But there is still a warm-up to come before the real joust. "It's obvious that Swifty is paying," says Romanoff, lighting his cigarette with a solid gold Dunhill. "Look how you're seated."

"You are admitting that Swifty wouldn't have had this table without us," snaps Bogart.

"I meant nothing of the kind," says Romanoff blandly.

"But your meaning was clear," insists Bogart. "Swifty may be one of your best customers but he would never have had this table if he was not dining with us."

Mrs. Bogart, who was thoroughly enjoying the warm-up, interrupts to announce the arrival of their host, Irving Paul Lazar, who is known variously as Swifty and Ipl, as in "Ripple." Swifty is as short as Romanoff but is built like a miniature fullback. In dress a dandy, too, he has a smooth, cherubic face—Irwin Shaw once said he resembles a new kind of beach boy turned out by an expensive sporting goods store. Writer Richard Gehman has said that Swifty seems destined to go down in history as the most preposterously successful Hollywood literary agent of all time, and one of the most delightfully preposterous characters in a community where preposterousness is well-nigh obligatory.

Swifty follows the Hollywood practice of kissing Mrs. Bogart on both cheeks, a greeting once reserved by European royalty for equals. Only the reigning Hollywood queens of the day like Mrs. Bogart, Joan Crawford, Bette Davis, and Judy Garland offer both cheeks to be kissed. Lesser luminaries expect to be kissed on one cheek only. Handshaking is for inferiors, and the lower on the caste system the shakee the fewer the number of fingers given for shaking. A tourist who insisted on shaking hands with Lazar, for example, would have gotten only the little finger of the left hand—the very least possible digital recognition.

"Hello, my love," says Mrs. Bogart.

"Here's our host! Hiya, Swifty," says Bogart.

"I thought you asked me for lunch," says Swifty, as he shakes hands with Romanoff, exposes his cuffs, and neatly adjusts the crease on his trousers prior to sitting down.

"Did I?" asks Bogart with surprise. "Well, then, it's Mike's check. He should pay anyway, after what he's been saying about you . . . that you wouldn't have this table if you weren't dining with us. You, one of the best customers this joint has! What do you think of that?"

"That's a lie," says Romanoff calmly, carefully selecting a filter cigarette from a gold cigarette case that matches his lighter.

"I don't care if it's a lie or not, I shall be delighted to pay," says Swifty cheerfully.

Bogart, who has been listening carefully for just these words but has been pretending to be unconcerned, suddenly excuses himself to go say hello to Sid and Judy, who have just come in.

Bogart halts the Lufts en route to their own table. "Hiya, Bogie, what's new?" says Luft, who has spent the evening before getting drunk with Bogart.

"Good afternoon," says Bogie, bowing formally to Miss Garland. (He does not favor the double-cheek kissing routine.) "I wondered if you would join us for lunch?"

The Lufts look toward the Bogart table and see Swifty, who waves rather painfully. "Swifty's buying again," says Sid Luft.

"That's right," says Bogart.

"I don't think the joke's funny any more," says Judy. "It's getting too old."

"Sure it is," says Bogart. "But it's the only joke we've got."

Back at the table Mrs. Bogart watches the Lufts and Bogie threading their way around tables, pausing to shake hands and acknowledge greetings, but obviously making a course for the Bogart booth.

"He's asked them over," she says.

"And I'm astonished to see they've accepted," says Romanoff.

"Well, what difference does it make," says Swifty. "Let him have his fun. When the check comes I'll sign his name."

This news does not please Mike, who says in a somewhat hollow voice, "Let's not have a row, that's all I ask."

"I'll not have a row with Bogie," Swifty promises. "He's my pal. Anyway, he doesn't believe in fighting any more. He's a new man since he married Betty." Swifty follows his complaint with a slight bow but gives away the fact that he is irritated by exchanging the pair of Ben Franklin-type half glasses on his nose for an identical pair that he takes from an inner coat pocket.

Mrs. Bogart acknowledges the compliment with a smile, then sighs at the sight of her husband with the Lufts in tow. "What a charmer," she says. "He doesn't remember we have an interview here in half an hour."

As the Lufts settle themselves into the booth Bogart explains to Swifty, "I told them that you insisted we all have lunch together."

"We really didn't want to barge in," said Luft, "but Bogie said you'd be sore if we said no."

"Delighted," says Swifty, trying to be genial. "Be my guests."

"The table is too small, Bogie," complains Mrs. Bogart.

"That's Mike's fault. Don't blame me," says Bogart.

Reinhardt, whose professional gaze has taken in the entire incident, unhappily asks if everyone is dining at the one booth.

"That's right," said Bogart, grinning as he meets the angry gaze of his spouse.

Everyone squeezes right around the circular table, but it is not large enough. Reinhardt brings a chair for the host, who now has to sit in the traffic outside of the crowded booth.

"Somehow we never manage to have a quiet lunch with you, Swifty," says Bogart cheerfully. "I don't know what it is. You don't plan ahead."

Romanoff, who is being edged out of the booth, rises. "If you'll excuse me," he says stiffly, "someone important has just come into the pub."

"Have them join us," says Bogart.

Reinhardt tries to make order of the chaos and finally manages to distribute the menus.

Swifty has been stiffed once more. His youthful face is angry, and Bogart is chuckling happily as he surveys his little kingdom.

At 1:30 when I arrived for my interview Bogart and Bacall were alone. "It's too peaceful around here," Bogie complained. "Can't get in a good fight any more. There's no more controversy."

Miss Bacall smiled and rolled her eyes ceilingward. "You came just a little too late, Joe," she said. "Bogie was doing his best to liven things up for you."

Bogie, who was looking thoughtfully at his Drambuie, turned to me and said, tentatively, "You know, motion picture directing is a highly overrated job. It's not difficult. Anyone could do it."

"Oh, no," said Betty. She foresaw how many friends this line would make.

"Go on," I said.

"It takes no talent to direct a film," continued Bogart. "The popular notion that directors rehearse lines and tell actors how to read them is nonsense. For example, while we were filming *We're No Angels* at Paramount I heard Mike Curtiz go up to Aldo Ray and say, 'When you smile you're a good actor. When you don't smile, you stink.' Is that directing?"

I took my note pad out and started to scribble. "I'm with you," I said.

Bogart pushed his drink aside. "The trouble is most critics can't tell the difference between a bad script, a bad actor, and a bad director. What burns me up is that when the actor is good, the director gets the credit, and when the actor is bad it's the actor who stinks. If he's bad why not blame the director?

"Take Marlon Brando, for example. He was good in *Streetcar* and *Waterfront* and Elia Kazan got the credit. Brando's been good in other things, too. He's bad only with a bad director."

"What do you think of producers?" I asked.

"In twenty years in Hollywood I've never been able to figure out what they do. I suppose they give the Green

Light. After they flash it they ought to go on a fishing trip until the picture is over. Everything would still end up fine."

Bogart paused to watch me scribble. "How're we doing?" he asked.

"We need a little more about directors," I said. "We can end with the quote about producers."

"There are only ten good directors in Hollywood," said Bogart. "There's John Huston, William Wyler, William Wilder, Edward Dmytryk, and John Ford, who's an in-and-outer. Wyler isn't sure of what he wants but invariably he gets it. Dmytryk and the others know what they want and go after it. But most directors don't know what they want and wouldn't know if it was good anyway."

"Who are the other five good directors?" I asked.

"I can't think of them at the moment," Bogart retorted. "Anyway, why let five more men get swelled heads. Besides I have to have someone to talk to at Romanoff's."

I made a mental calculation of the words I needed for a column and estimated that I had enough. "I think it'll work," I said to Bogart who went back to his drink, a pleased grin on his face.

"Now it's your turn, Betty," Bogie said. Nudging me under the table he added, "Betty's going to be immortalized —she's putting her footprints in Grauman's Chinese Theater next week."

"Congratulations," I said.

"Thank you," said Miss Bacall properly.

Bogart ignored the polite exchange and continued, "It used to be an honor—it was at least back in 1946 when I did it—but it doesn't mean a thing any more. It's just a publicity stunt for every starlet. It's no honor."

Betty looked a trifle pained but bravely picked up the thread of her husband's conversation. "You're right, I guess," she said. "They ask most everyone."

Bogie looked triumphant. "It's time someone spoke out about this phony practice," he said, his meaning all too clear.

"This is a very tricky area you're steering Betty into," I said. "Grauman's is an institution."

"Well, I don't know about that," said Betty, warming to the subject. "Before I came to Hollywood Grauman's Chinese was something very special to me. It meant not only achievement, but it was the hall of fame of the motion picture industry and the people in it were unforgettables and irreplaceables. I don't think of myself as either."

Bogart smiled on his spouse proudly and shoved my note pad under my nose. "You're not taking it down," he said.

Needled to the point of action, Betty, at Bogie's suggestion, went into Romanoff's accounting room and, borrowing a typewriter, wrote out a statement explaining why she would not put her footprints in the cement forecourt of Grauman's Chinese Theater.

She returned fifteen minutes later and read the statement to us. Bogie nodded approvingly, suggested a few minor changes, and gave it to me.

"I guess I've blown my chance at immortality," Betty said, as I pocketed her statement.

"It's time someone spoke out," said Bogie, happily.

The joint interview was over. Typical of all my interviews with the Bogarts either alone or together, it was fun to do as well as fun to read.

None of the Bogarts' friends stopped by our table to kid around or say good-bye. Bogart would not have tolerated any interruption. When he gave an interview he was as coolly professional as on the set. "If I'm going to spend my time talking to someone for publication, it's as much my job as standing in front of the cameras," he told me. "And I work just as hard at it."

It was 3:30 in the afternoon and the main dining room was empty when both interviews were concluded. Mike came by the table to show Bogie the luncheon bill. It was for $96.00.

"Note here," said Mike, pointing to the signature.

Swifty had signed: Humphrey Bogart.

Bogie laughed. "It's a forgery, Mike, and you know it," he said.

"All I know is that it says 'Humphrey Bogart' and that's who is going to get the bill," said Mike.

"Anyone can come in here and sign my name and I get the bill, is that what you're saying?" said Bogie.

Mike said nothing, but there was an amused gleam in his eyes.

"Then I'll sign Swifty's name to the tab next time," said Bogie gleefully—as he initialed the bill: "OK H.B."

The "only joke we've got" had been expanded to a new joke.

But a bigger joke had its inception a few nights later

when David and Hjordis Niven, Mike Romanoff, Irving Lazar, Frank Sinatra, Judy Garland and Sid Luft, James Van Heusen, Nathaniel Benchley, and the Bogarts assembled for dinner in Mike's posh upstairs room. Betty Bacall looked around at the group of adult, overprivileged delinquents, and cracked, "I see the rat pack is all here."

Something about the name, Rat Pack, intrigued the group. After a few hours of drinking they decided to form an organization with a platform of iconoclasm—they were against everything and everyone, including themselves.

I got wind of the meeting the next day and called Bogie. "News must be pretty tight when you start to cover parties at Romanoff's," he said.

"It sounds like fun," I answered.

"That's what it was and you'll blow it up out of all proportion," he said.

"I'll handle it straight, and it will be all the funnier," I promised.

Bogie thought that over for a minute and admitted that so treated the story could be humorous. "Remember, though, it was all a joke," he said.

The first official notice of the Rat Pack appeared the next day in my column in the New York *Herald Tribune*.

The Holmby Hills Rat Pack held its first annual meeting last night at Romanoff's restaurant in Beverly Hills and elected officers for the coming year. Named to executive positions were: Frank Sinatra, pack master; Judy Garland, first vice president; Lauren Bacall, den mother; Sid Luft, cage master; Humphrey Bogart, rat in charge of public relations; Irving Lazar, recording secretary and treasurer; Nathaniel Benchley, historian.

The only members of the organization not voted into office are David Niven, Michael Romanoff and James Van Heusen. Mr. Niven, an Englishman, Mr. Romanoff, a Russian, and Mr. Van Heusen, an American, protested that they were discriminated against because of their national origins. Mr. Sinatra, who was acting chairman of the meeting, refused to enter their protests on the minutes.

A coat of arms designed by Mr. Benchley was unanimously approved as the official insignia of the Holmby Hills Rat Pack for use on letterheads and membership pins. The escutcheon features a rat gnawing on a human hand with a legend, "Never Rat on a Rat."

Mr. Bogart, who was spokesman, said the organization has no specific function other than "the relief of boredom and the perpetuation of independence. We admire ourselves and don't care for anyone else."

He said that membership is open to free-minded, successful individuals who don't care what anyone thinks about them.

A motion concerning the admittance of Claudette Colbert was tabled at the insistence of Miss Bacall who said that Miss Colbert "is a nice person but not a rat."

The Rat Pack started out as a casual joke, but it soon became part of the Hollywood culture. Actually it was just a name for an amorphous group of Hollywood celebrities, friends of the Bogarts, who met at Romanoff's for lunch whenever possible or convened convivially at the Bogart house two or three evenings a week. Usually they just sat around and talked, though sometimes Judy Garland or Frank Sinatra would sing with composers James Van Heusen or Sammy Cahn at the piano. They all stayed up late and drank a good deal when not working. Sometimes there were loud arguments, mainly political, which delighted Bogart. Sometimes he managed to initiate a fight, which pleased him even more.

Although Bogart was officially only the Director of Public Relations, as the driving force in Hollywood society in those days he was the Pack's acknowledged leader.

EIGHT

Early in 1946 Bogie negotiated a new contract with Jack L. Warner in a ten-minute telephone conversation leaving his salary to be negotiated. Mary Baker was present at the first meeting between Bogie's agent, Sam Jaffe (Mary Baker's partner) and the studio head. Jaffe tentatively suggested a salary of $125,000. Mr. Warner smiled. Jaffe hastily concluded the meeting. Outside Warner's door, Mary asked the agent why he didn't finish the negotiations. "J. L. was smiling when we mentioned $125,000," the agent said. "I think we ought to ask for more money." "How much more?" Mary asked. "Enough at least to make the man frown," said Jaffe.

Weeks later when Bogart went to sign the contract he was wearing an ill-fitting toupee: All of his hair except for one sideburn and one eyebrow had fallen out in patches as a result of hormone treatments. For the first time he wanted to have children.

Warner, who had heard rumors that Bogart was going bald, eyed the toupee suspiciously but said nothing. Later, however, he telephoned Mary Baker to ask if the rumors were true. Mary admitted they were. Warner was in a panic. "Good God!" he said. "Some leading man I've signed up! He has hardly a hair on his head."

The hair began to grow back as it had fallen out—in patches. Warner had his star again, but with a most unusual contract. The brief conversation between actor and studio head had become a ninety-page legal document that guaranteed, among other things, that Bogart was to do one picture a year for a salary of $200,000. He could reject two out of three stories submitted to him, but he either took the third or furnished his own story. He could turn down any director he didn't like with the exception of five whom he had approved when he signed the contract. He also was allowed to do one outside film for himself each year. The contract was to run for fifteen years guaranteeing him $3,000,000 and the right to do outside films.

It also specified that Bogart was to receive $1,000 a week for living expenses when on location; he was to be given roundtrip tickets from Los Angeles to all locations for his family and one other person of his choosing—usually a hairdresser-secretary who handled his "rug" (toupee), answered mail, and mixed drinks; he had approval of all publicity releases on his pictures and the right to approve all photographs taken of him before release to the press (again, the toupee was his main concern).

There were other inclusions tailored to his personal taste: He was to quit work at 6 P.M. daily (thus allowing himself time for a drink after work), and there was a paragraph devoted to the size and furnishings of his dressing rooms at the studio and on location, with a mention that each was to be equipped with an ice box.

"Whenever we'd move or change locations, the thing of importance was not the script or costume but 'Where the hell's the ice box?'" said Bob Schiffler, Bogie's sailing companion and makeup man.

Bogie had the right to select his own makeup man, and whenever Schiffler was available he went on Bogart's pictures. "I told him many times he didn't need makeup," Schiffler said. "He was never concerned about his looks, but he liked to have me around and I liked to be with him."

Bogart had finally achieved a position of real eminence at his home studio. In 1946, the first year of his contract, his income according to the Treasury Department was $432,000. After nine suspensions at Warner's—taken because he held out for better parts—he was on his way professionally to being what he had been privately all along: his own man.

"When I was coming up, the studio used me as a threat to the top boys: Muni, Raft, Cagney, Robinson," Bogart told reporter Philip K. Scheur. "When Muni, Cagney, and Robinson left I was moved ahead. They had to have a new 'he man.' Now they use Johnny Garfield and Bernie Zanville—what's his new name? Dane Clark—to keep me in line.

"All the studios do it. They have to protect their investments. They can make anyone a star if they get behind him. That's why I don't kid myself, why I can't take myself—or the business—seriously.

"What is my business? Acting. I'm an actor. I do my job like you do yours. If I'm a good actor, so much the better. A good actor can have a bad part and get by. If he gets a good part, he's all set. I was just as good when I did *Swing Your Lady*—my worst picture—as I am today, but the studio wasn't behind me then."

His tremendous income gave Bogart the financial security he wanted and considered important for just one reason—to enable him to tell the studio to go to hell. "Nobody can be a good actor without a sense of truth, of right and wrong," he told some young actors at his house one night. "If you want to be an actor, be honest with yourself. Don't let them push you around. When you believe in something, you fight for it, even though you may suffer for it. We actors are better judges than any studio as to what is good for us. As soon as your name gets known and you feel you can say, 'I won't do this,' if you think the part isn't right—go ahead and say it. In the long run it will pay off. Just remember to put some dough aside for the times you're suspended."

After *To Have and Have Not*, Bogie worked with Bacall again in *The Big Sleep*, in which he played Raymond Chandler's tough private eye, Philip Marlowe. Chandler was delighted with Bogart in the role. "Bogart can be tough without a gun," the author said. "Also, he has a sense of humor that contains that grating undertone of contempt. Alan Ladd is hard, bitter, and occasionally charming, but he is after all a small boy's idea of a tough guy. Bogart is the genuine article. Like Edward G. Robinson, all he has to do to dominate a scene is to enter it."

Howard Hawks, who directed both pictures with Lauren Bacall, said Bogart was extremely easy to work with. "He was really underrated as an actor. Without his help I couldn't have done what I did with Bacall. Not many actors would sit around and wait while a girl steals a scene. But he fell in love with the girl and the girl with him, and that made it easy."

"I don't believe in competitive acting," Bogie once told me. "I remember Alfred Lunt once said that he didn't either. 'If I did,' Lunt said, 'Lynn and I would have to be billed as Lunt vs. Fontanne.'"

In 1947 "B and B," as the fan magazines now called them,

did *Dark Passage* together, a well-made potboiler about a man unjustly imprisoned for murder who escapes to catch the real killer—played by Bruce Bennett.

Then Bogie worked without Betty but with a superb cast including Walter Huston, Bruce Bennett, and Tim Holt in *The Treasure of the Sierra Madre*, directed by Walter Huston's son, John. The film was made on location in San José de Purua, an isolated village about 140 miles north of Mexico City. The life was rugged, with burning sun, tropical downpours, steep hills, assorted insects and reptiles, and bad meals. Lauren, who accompanied Bogie on the trip, made regular trips to the kitchen to prepare ham and eggs for him.

Director Huston, who was a stickler for authenticity, soon earned the nickname of "Hard-Way Huston." "John wanted everything perfect," Bogart said. "If he saw a nearby mountain that could serve for photographic purposes, that mountain was no good: too easy to reach. If we could get to a location site without fording a couple of streams and walking through snake-infested areas in the scorching sun, then it wasn't quite right."

Bogart and John Huston got along wonderfully well until the end of the picture. Then Huston decreed some extra scenes that lengthened the schedule, and this caused Bogie to miss taking part in the Honolulu race with his new yacht, *Santana.* "We had a terrible row and were sore as hell at each other for days," said Huston. "Then we had a few drinks of an ancient tequila laced with Scotch—his favorite local beverage—and anger melted into understanding and then sympathy."

The Hustons, father and son, got Oscars for their work and Bogart only got an Academy Award nomination. But his performance as a trigger-happy prospector in the Mexican hills who gets his just deserts was memorable. "Nobody gets the best of Fred C. Dobbs," he said, and very few actors did.

At a post-Oscar celebration at Huston's house, Bogie and his host, with a pet monkey clinging to his neck, engaged in a football game against movie executive Collier Young and writer Charles Grayson. The game was played in the mud with a genuine Ming vase for a ball and with producer Henry Blanke and Betty as referees. The players were wearing tuxedos. The spirit of competition was so keen that two of Young's ribs were fractured. Ida Lupino, who was then married to Mr. Young, decided to get into the proceedings and sprained her back.

Bogie's next film with Betty was *Key Largo,* with Edward G. Robinson, Lionel Barrymore, and Claire Trevor, again directed by John Huston. The Maxwell Anderson melodrama of a disillusioned veteran facing gangsterism on a Florida key was a moody, compact, and exciting film. Bogart was completely at home in the sort of reluctant-hero role that came easily to him. "His loneliness was based on suspicions of everyone's motives, and the statement of this fact was the everlasting theme of his life's work," wrote Richard Shickel. "It accounted for his defensive inwardness, his unbreakable facade."

Claire Trevor got an Oscar for her role in *Key Largo,* but Bogart got the reviews.

Since he was allowed to make pictures on his own, at a time when all Hollywood stars were working for their own companies with an eye toward building up capital gains, Bogart formed Santana Productions with Robert Lord and Mark Hellinger as partners. The first Santana picture was *Knock on Any Door.* Nick Ray directed Bogart as a lawyer who defends slum kid John Derek in a murder trial. Other Santana Productions made for Columbia release between 1949 and 1951 included *Tokyo Joe, In a Lonely Place,* and *Sirocco.*

Of the first batch of his own films, Bogart told Howard Thompson of *The New York Times:* "*Knock on Any Door* was good but could have been better and set us up on our feet because it made money. We made it for $900,000 plus 25% overhead. *Tokyo Joe* made money, too. *Sirocco* was one we had to do, and it stank, of course."

Bogart neglected to mention *In a Lonely Place,* which he didn't like, though the critics considered it the best of his early independent films. The moody melodrama about an eccentric screenwriter who finds happiness briefly with Gloria Grahame and then almost kills her caught much of the cruelty, edginess, and sentimentality of Hollywood. It was directed by Nick Ray, who was then married to Miss Grahame.

Then one day in 1950 John Huston called Bogie on the telephone. "I have a great story," Huston said. "The hero is a lowlife. You are the biggest lowlife in town and therefore most suitable for the part."

Enchanted by Huston's novel pitch, Bogart suggested that they drink lunch at Romanoff's. The upshot of the meeting was that they both rushed over to call on Katharine

Hepburn and reveal to her the enticements of an incredible story about a skinny missionary spinster and a sweet-water rumpot who float down an African river to fire a homemade torpedo at a German gunboat.

The improbable tale, written by C. S. Forester and published in 1935, had been owned by both Warner's and Twentieth Century-Fox before Sam Spiegel bought it and interested Huston. The big studios were averse to producing the film because of the high cost of the location.

Finally it was decided to go ahead, and Bogie, accompanied by Betty, started off for Africa via New York. One night when Betty went to bed early, Bogie, accompanied by Quentin Reynolds, stopped in at the Stork Club for a nightcap. Sherman Billingsley, the proprietor, asked Bogie to appear on his television program.

Bogart said, "I'm sorry. I wear a wig for professional appearances and I haven't got it with me."

Billingsley persisted. He said it didn't matter—after all he wore one himself. "Look," said Bogart, "I can't go on a TV screen like this. I'm known as a screen lover. That sort of type." And he added with a straight face, "Not like you."

That did it. Billingsley flushed angrily. Bogie, enjoying the effect of the needling, then told Billingsley straight out that he didn't want to appear on the show, that he considered it a bore, anyway, and wouldn't appear on it under any circumstances.

"Then you'd better get out of my restaurant," said Billingsley.

"You mean I'm barred," said Bogart, his reaction somewhat less penitent than might have been expected.

"The challengers will never overtake me now," he announced happily to writer George Frazier. "I still have several more days to go in New York and feel with a little effort on my part I can probably get barred from Central Park and Ebbets Field. As a matter of fact, the only places I am really socially acceptable now are "21" and Grand Central Station. Put it down to natural charm. I'm loaded with it. And experience, too. You don't get to be the Boris Karloff of the supper clubs overnight. You've got to work at it."

A few days later Bogie and Betty arrived in London to discover that there were complications with the film. Sam Spiegel's backers had backed out. Spiegel persuaded Bogie to invest in the film himself. Bogart, Huston, and Hepburn deferred their salaries in order to get it made. Miss Hepburn made only one condition: that Spiegel pay their hotel bills as he had agreed. "I didn't mind doing the film for nothing, but I didn't intend to pay money for the privilege of doing it," Miss Hepburn said.

The film, *The African Queen,* was shot almost entirely in the most inaccessible spots Huston could find in the Belgian Congo and Uganda. Everyone came down with dysentery except Betty and Bogie, who avoided drinking any water— he even brushed his teeth with Scotch.

When they began the film, Miss Hepburn, who was convinced that Bogart was a profligate, lectured him and Huston on the evils of drinking—although without drinking neither of them could have endured life on the Ruiki River. When she finished her sermon, Bogie said, "Fine, fine, Katie. Now get yourself a chair, pull one up for me, and fix the drinks." Such was Bogie's charm that Miss Hepburn did as she was told.

One night the camp was attacked by an army of soldier ants. Bogie, with drink in hand, sallied out to cheer on the crew who were burning oil and yelling, trying to divert the column. Miss Hepburn, who with Betty had discovered the ants earlier in the day, came out on the balcony of her bungalow and verbally lambasted Bogart in ringing tones for staging a drunken brawl in the middle of the night.

"Bogie was wonderful," recalled Huston. "With simple dignity he explained to her, 'Katie, old girl. Ants.' "

Bogart used to take a siesta on a hammock set up on a raft in the river. He boasted that the mosquitoes bit him, then rolled over dead or drunk. "His strength was in Scotch," Huston said. "I think all of us were ill in some way or another, but not Bogie."

The African safari was rugged in every respect, and Bogart griped and griped but worked and worked. "But what exasperated him most," said Huston, "was Katie Hepburn's calm acceptance of the heat and the damp and the stinks and the crawling life of the jungle."

"Damn Hepburn! Damn her, she's so goddam cheerful," Bogie exploded one afternoon. "She's got ants in her pants, mildew in her shoes, and she's still cheerful. I build a solid wall of whiskey between me and the bugs. She doesn't drink, and she breezes through it all as though it was a weekend in Connecticut!"

The old boat they used in *The African Queen* sprang a leak one day and settled to the bottom of the river deep in the African jungle. It took five days to raise it. Meanwhile, the English engineer who had kept the temperamental boiler perking had packed up and left the movie troupe. "John was delighted," said Bogie. "He had a real crisis. My only crisis was the time the party ran out of Scotch for two days."

Although in the retelling Bogart's adventures seemed mostly concerned with his favorite beverage, he assured me once that the entire picture was a labor of love. "We loved those two silly people on that boat," he said. "And Katie, of course, was absolutely perfect."

Perfect as Miss Hepburn was, it was Bogart who got the Oscar this time. On the night he was announced as Best Actor for 1951, Bogart kissed Betty and jauntily walked up to the stage of the Pantages Theater. Once in front of the imposing audience of his peers, however, he fluffed his carefully prepared ad lib and stammered a polite thanks. Backstage in the press tent where Oscar winners are photographed and interviewed he recovered his Bogartism in time to proclaim that it was all bunk, that the only true test of ability would be to have all the actors don black tights and recite Hamlet. But there was a happy gleam in his eyes as he hefted the seven-pound, gold-plated, sixty-four-dollar statuette that purports to prove that the recipient is the best film actor of the year.

That night at a party in Romanoff's upstairs Crown Room Bogart was square again as he modestly acknowledged the toasts. "He was terribly pleased because he didn't think he would win," said Adolph Green, recalling that was a year that saw Marlon Brando and Montgomery Clift set the two basic styles for modern acting in *A Streetcar Named Desire* and *A Place in the Sun*.

The next morning son Steve, then three, brought Bogie back to earth when he seized the Oscar and hurled it at his parent. Bogart spent the day relishing a spate of telegrams from such friends as Spencer Tracy, John O'Hara, Louis Bromfield, Henry Blanke, and Miss Hepburn. All the messages were properly derogatory.

"The way to survive an Oscar," Bogart told columnist Erskine Johnson a few days later, "is to never try to win another one. You've seen what happens to some Oscar winners. They spend the rest of their lives turning down scripts while searching for the great role to win another one. Hell, I hope I'm never even nominated again. It's meat-and-potatoes roles for me from now on."

One day while making *The African Queen*, John Huston had tossed a book to Bogart written by an Irishman named James Helvick. The title was *Beat the Devil*. "We might make a picture of this sometime," Huston said offhandedly. Bogart read it and agreed with him. It was a good book with some wonderful bits about a Spanish official whose big problem in life was deciding whether it was more chic to drive a Rolls-Royce or a Cadillac. There was also some good material about the way a woman's lies confuse a bunch of cutthroats.

Knowing Huston liked the book but had no money of his own, Bogart bought it when he got back to the States. He called Huston in Paris to tell him they owned the property. "Let's go to work on it," Huston said. "I'll get the author to come here and we'll do the screenplay."

Bogart didn't hear a word for weeks, then got a cable: "Author impoverished. Need money. Expedite cash."

Later, Bogart learned that the author really was broke, which was what interested John in doing the picture in the first place. They were neighbors in Ireland, and he wanted to help him out.

Faced with the business of getting a screenplay, Huston and Bogart hired two writers who worked three months in collaboration: Peter Viertel in Switzerland and Tony Veiller in Venice working with Huston in Ireland.

Meanwhile, Bogart was still interested in "meat-and-potatoes" roles. Immediately after returning from Africa he played a tough-minded managing editor for Twentieth Century-Fox in *Deadline, U.S.A.*, then went over to MGM to become a tough fibered army medico in *Battle Circus*. Both pictures were directed by Richard Brooks, a new young writer Bogart liked.

Then Bogart finally parted company with Warner Brothers. Although his fabulous contract still had eight years to run, he had not been able to come to terms on a story at the studio since *The Enforcer*, a routine melodrama made in 1950, and he didn't want to hold himself available to Warner's for six months a year.

Warner agreed to the parting, and Bogart revived his own independent company, Santana, for *Beat the Devil*, which then had a starting date in London. Bogart arrived on time and found, waiting for him, a script that Huston had sent from Paris. He later told me, "I couldn't finish reading it. It was awful."

Next day he got a call from Huston, who cheerfully asked if he had read the script. "Couldn't read it," said Bogart.

"Neither could I," said Huston. "Stinker, isn't it? See you in Rome tomorrow."

The following afternoon they were sitting in George's American Bar in back of the Excelsior Hotel in Rome having tea when a man tossed a copy of *Daily Variety,* the film trade paper, on their table.

The first four pages were devoted exclusively to the revolution in Hollywood: Flat pictures were out, black-and-white films were passé, 3-D was the coming process. Their picture was going to be two-dimensional and black-and-white.

It was a crisis. Huston looked at Bogart. Bogart looked at Huston. They ordered double martinis.

"There we were in Rome with a no-good script and a picture which *Variety* said would die at birth," said Bogart. "We cabled the States to try and borrow a 3-D lens. Meanwhile we were getting cables from David O. Selznick, whose wife Jennifer Jones was going to be in the picture. 'Abandon project. Take one of mine,' he wired. 'You'll ruin your career and Jennifer's.' "

Bogart and Huston found they couldn't work in Rome so they went to Rapallo on the Mediterranean. "We both had terrible colds and naturally took the prescribed cure," said Bogart. "It worked wonders. In three days the colds were gone and Huston had an idea."

"We'll get Truman Capote to write the screenplay," he said. "Instead of trying to do *Casablanca* and *Maltese Falcon* over again we'll make it a human picture with lots of heart and humor."

Capote turned out to be magnificent. He wrote like fury with an upside-down slant on humor. They cabled Jennifer Jones to come at once, hired Gina Lollobrigida and Peter Lorre, and began to look for an Italian crew and cast. The Italian actors had to learn their lines phonetically, and they used translators to relay Huston's instructions to the crew. Huston speaks not a word in any language but his own: He has complete disregard for any tongue except English.

Just before the picture started Huston and Bogart drove to Rome from Naples with a chauffeur and an ancient car. They were in the back of the car asleep when suddenly a divider island loomed up in the middle of the road. The driver apparently couldn't decide which branch to take. He drove straight ahead through two stone walls that completely demolished the car and considerably rattled the bones of its occupants.

Bogie was thrown forward and hit the front seat. Blood gushed from his mouth. He had bitten right through his tongue and loosened two teeth. "Bad luck," he mumbled, "just when we've started the picture."

When they got to Naples they ran into George Sanders and told him Bogart's problem. Sanders took him to a German doctor who said, "Lie down. The point of the needle to anesthetize will hurt as much as the point of the needle to sew up the tongue, so we will eliminate it. Have courage, be of good faith." He stitched up the tongue without anesthesia.

Although one tooth wobbled thereafter (all of his teeth were finally capped), they were at work within a week. "Bogie had guts," Huston commented on the incident. "Not bravura. Real courage."

The work schedule on the picture was rigorous, but Huston and Bogart worked all day and played poker all night: They had hired Bob Capa to shoot the stills and their goal was to get their money back from him. Also, they wanted to get the money that Jennifer cost them back from Selznick, who was on the location. Luckily, Capa was the worst poker player in the world, but he beat out Selznick for the title by only a small margin. Capote tried to play poker, but what with the death of his pet raven, an abscessed tooth, and only being a day and a half ahead of the shooting schedule he was pretty tired. They took a couple of hundred thousand lira from him and told him to stay home and sleep nights.

Bogart and Capote became good friends, however, making a combination that amused themselves as well as their contemporaries.

"The turning point in our friendship, the beginning really, was during the film while Bogie and some others were arm wrestling," Capote told writer Peter Bogdanovich. "Well, it just happens that I'm very good at that game. So anyway, Bogie called over, 'Hey, Caposy'—that's what he called me—'let's see you try this.' And I went over and pushed his arm down. Well, he looked at me. . . . He had such a suspicious mind, he was sure that Huston had cut off my head and sewed it onto someone else's body. 'Let's see you do that again,' he said. And again I pushed his arm down. So he said once more, and I said I would only if we bet a hundred dollars, which we did. I won again and he paid me, but then he came over and started sort of semiwrestling with me. It was something they did. He was crushing me and I said 'Cut that out,' and he said, 'Why?' I said, 'Because you're hurting me.' But he kept right on squeezing, so I got my leg around behind him and pushed and over he went. He was flat on his can looking up at me. And from then on we were very good friends."

A few weeks after *Beat the Devil* was released Bogart telephoned me to say he had a story for me. Could I lunch with him at Romanoff's at 12:30?

"Who's paying?" I asked.

"You pay for yourself," Bogart said. "Put it on your expenses—I have a good story for you."

When I arrived at about 12:31 Bogart was waiting and anxiously glancing at his watch. Without pausing for the usual insults he thrust an ad from a newspaper in front of me. "Read this," he said.

The ad was on the entertainment page of the *Evening News*, Sault Sainte Marie, Michigan. Under the listing of *Beat the Devil* was this message from the theater management: "Personally if you don't see this picture you are not missing much. The picture at The Temple did not come up to our expectations. We would like to discontinue it, but are forced to play it until Wednesday. Please accept our apologies. After the first show tonight we will give passes to the first ten people who tell us they actually liked it."

"You saw the picture—you said you liked it," said Bogart, snatching the ad back from me.

"Yeah, but it's a long way to go to get a free pass," I said.

"Very funny," said Bogart, who handed me a letter from John Huston that read: "Enclosed please find several letters from grateful customers and also grateful exhibitors who have been privileged to exhibit and see 'the thing.' As you can see by the ads the exhibitors are behind us all the way. I'm afraid too far behind, say about $1,000,000. In spite of all this it looks as though we'll just about scrape through and to cheer you up I met a weird character the other day who almost knocked me down screaming, 'But I liked it, I liked it!' "

The letters were as witty as they were caustic. I asked Bogie if he wanted me to run them. "Hell, no," he said, "I didn't bring you here to knock the picture. I want to do a piece knocking exhibitors. What burns me up is we risked a great deal of money to make this picture. I put in about $400,000 of my own money, and I don't think there's an exhibitor in the business who would risk five cents of his money in a film.

"I never heard of an exhibitor buying a book and saying to a producer, 'Here's a picture I suggest you make.' Instead they sit on their asses and criticize creative people who invest their own time, talent, and money making a picture that the exhibitor—the parasite of the film business—can make money with."

Bogart carried on in this vituperative vein for twenty minutes, carefully supervised my note taking, and asked me to read the quotes back to him. Then he asked how I planned to handle the story. Apparently satisfied, he devoted himself to ham and eggs, black coffee, and a heated argument with Mike Romanoff, who claimed that humanity created God in its own image and then proceeded to kill Him. Bogart disputed the point, revealing a surprisingly religious attitude.

When I left the table, Bogart said, "See if you can get the quotes exact for a change."

"If I quoted you exactly no one would print it," I said.

Two days later Bogart telephoned me again. "I don't know why the hell I let you talk me into things," he said. "I've been on the phone all morning with exhibitors who are furious at that blast I let you con me into making." Before I could rise to my defense he added slyly, "It was a good piece, kid. Looks like we told them off, huh?"

NINE

One day I asked Bogart who he thought was the best actor in Hollywood. "I am Number One," he said kiddingly. "Spencer Tracy is Number Two." Some time later I asked Tracy the same question. "I am Number One," he said, a mischievous gleam in his eye. "Bogart is Number Two."

Many producers tried to team the two old friends and mutual admirers together, but the billing always proved to be an insuperable obstacle. "I'd have lunch with Bogie and show him on paper all kinds of double acrostics in which his name crossed Tracy's," said Irving Lazar, who tried to arrange a deal for *Desperate Hours*. "All the juggling tricks. But neither of them would give up top billing, so they never made a picture together."

Bogart and Tracy were, as Katharine Hepburn once said, branches from the same rugged oak. They were real stars. "The phrase 'movie star' is misused so much that it has no real meaning any more," Bogart once told me. "Any little pinhead who makes one picture is called a star. In my book, Gable is a star; Cooper and Tracy are stars; and, as much as I dislike the lady, Joan Crawford is a star. To be a star you have to drag your weight in the box office and be recognized wherever you go.

"Do you know why I'm worth $200,000 a picture? Not just because I can get it but because people like my face. Little kids with money in their hot little fists like it; old women like it. I have the greatest following of children up to eight years old and over sixty of any actor in Hollywood. The old

137

women are grateful because they remember me twenty years ago. Once they're gone I won't get $200,000 a picture."

Actually, Bogart was probably the lowest-paid top star of his time. "He didn't drive the hardest bargain," said Swifty Lazar. "He put up his own money if he wanted to do a picture. Frank Sinatra will say, 'I want to do this picture,' and then send his lawyers to say Frank wants a million dollars for this picture he is so crazy about. Not Bogie. Any good director could get him for nothing. All the other actors say they'll work for nothing—but that's a lot of nonsense. If a producer or director needed money Bogie would give it to them. That's the kind of cat he was, as he proved on *African Queen* and *Beat the Devil*."

Bogart was also the kind of cat who didn't care when he heard that Edward Dmytryk, who had served a prison sentence for contempt of court as one of "The Hollywood Ten," had been set to direct *The Caine Mutiny* for Stanley Kramer. "I don't give a damn what his politics were," Bogart said. "He satisfied the government that he's OK now, and that satisfies me."

Bogart wanted the role of Captain Queeg badly and competed against almost every other major star in Hollywood for it. Stanley Kramer, the producer, chose Bogart because he felt he was physically perfect and he liked his approach to the role.

Bogart planned to breathe his own brand of fire into Captain Queeg, the stormy heavy of Herman Wouk's best-selling novel. When Columbia executives complained to Bogart that he was not making Captain Queeg crazy enough, Bogart defended his interpretation to a reporter: "That's not the way I see Queeg and it's not the way I'll play him. Queeg was not crazy, he was sick. I don't know whether he was a schizophrenic, a manic depressive or a paranoiac—I'm not smart about those things—but I do know that a person who has any of these things works overtime at being normal. In fact, he's supernormal until he's pressured. Then he blows up.

"I personally know a Queeg in every studio in Hollywood —not necessarily the head man."

The executives shut up.

Bob Yeager who was press agent on *The Caine Mutiny* still relishes the day when Bogart was filming the strawberry scene on the sound stage in Hollywood. "The scene started when Van Johnson came in to tell Captain Queeg (Bogart) about the missing keys and strawberries. Edward Dmytryk, the director, thought it would be better if Bogie was busy doing something during the scene. He decided Bogie should butter some toast.

"We had a technical director from the navy, a Commander Shaw, on the picture. All during the scene when Bogie was buttering the toast Commander Shaw was mumbling. Finally, he said that Bogie was breaking off too big a piece of toast.

" 'A naval officer and gentleman would not break off such big pieces,' he told Kramer. He insisted that Bogie be corrected, or the scene wouldn't be passed in Washington.

"When Bogie was told the news his face clouded over angrily. 'I am more of a gentleman and know more about manners than any Annapolis man,' he told Commander Shaw. 'You just stick to worrying about the buttons on the uniforms and leave the acting alone.'

"The next time they did the scene, Bogie broke off a piece of bread the size of his thumbnail and elaborately lathered it with butter. Commander Shaw almost had apoplexy, but he kept his mouth shut."

Some time later I went to Hawaii during the filming of *The Caine Mutiny*. Bogart was there with Betty and Stephen. He had worked all week in a role that consumed most of his thought and energy and he generally disliked discussing his roles, but this day he talked about Queeg, as we sat on the lanai of the Royal Hawaiian Hotel.

"Queeg was not a sadist," he said. "He was not a cruel man, he was a very sick man. His was a life of frustrations and insecurity. His victories were always small victories. He made the men stick their shirttails in and he cleaned up the ship. But when he was faced with a real problem—the typhoon, for example—he cracked up so badly that Lieutenant Maryk (Van Johnson), his second in command, felt it necessary to take over the ship. In peacetime Queeg was a capable officer, but he could not stand the stress of war." Bogart paused, then added, "I knew men like him during the last war. I understand him."

That was about as close as Bogart ever came to a serious discussion of any character he played. Later, when someone asked him how he had his eyes look crazy in the courtroom scene in *Caine*, he said, "It was easy. I'm nuts, you know." And he eventually admitted that he didn't think the film was so hot. "It was crapped up with an unnecessary love story," he explained, and said that he regarded *The African Queen* as his best picture.

Once, in a discussion of acting with some young actors for *Look*, Bogart said, "Acting has nothing to do with vanity. It's the satisfaction it provides—like telling a joke and having everybody laugh. I have a charming wife, two beautiful kids, a gorgeous home, a yacht—and I've had the applause. I'll be damned if I know why I work so hard. Work is therapy, I guess. It keeps me on the wagon. This is a very bad town to be out of work in. After a week or so of not working, you're so bored you don't know what the hell to do."

He concluded the interview by saying, "If you do want to be an actor, don't say, 'I want to be a star'—just concentrate on acting; learn your trade. You've got to develop confidence if you're to play a scene right, and confidence comes from knowing the ropes."

Bogart was intensely, passionately professional about his work. Nunnally Johnson still recalls Bogart's explosion when he heard some of his colleagues apologizing for being film stars. "Dammit," Bogart said, "I don't approve of these bums saying, 'I'm no actor. I just act natural.' If they aren't film actors what the hell are they paid for?"

Acting was, as Truman Capote once said, almost the sum total of Bogart's life. "He was really an artist and a very selective one. All the gestures and expressions were pruned down and pruned down."

Nowhere was this professionalism more visible than when Bogart played a role that he disliked or for which he felt unfitted, as in *Sabrina*, which followed *The Caine Mutiny*.

In *Sabrina* he played a wealthy Wall Street type, complete with Homburg, furled black umbrella, Brooks Brothers suit and briefcase—all the regalia to which he was born but despised on principle. And he got the girl, Audrey Hepburn, edging out Bill Holden. Bogart didn't like the picture. He was not fond of Holden, whom he considered the apotheosis of the "boy next door," and of Audrey Hepburn he scathingly said, "She's all right if you don't mind a dozen takes."

When some reviewers complained, however, that it didn't seem logical that he and not Holden got the girl, Bogart attacked became Bogart the attacker. "That talk I shouldn't get the girl is insulting," he said. "One of the things that Hollywood does is bury you after you reach the age of Tony Curtis. The tombstone is already up. This is a funny American idea. In Europe you don't run into that problem."

The fact is the critics had touched a sensitive nerve. Despite his popularity Bogart felt he had only a brief time left on the screen before the younger actors shoved him out of the way. He was not soothed by the fact that he was getting more and better parts than at any time in his career.

"He had the occupational insecurity of most actors," Betty told me. "He was never sure when he would work again. He was always talking about 'something to leave' for me and the kids. For that reason nearly all the picture deals he made were negotiated with that in mind."

Like most top stars Bogart was an employee of his own company, and when he worked on a picture the company was paid for his services. When the company and its interest in his films were sold the money would be a capital gain and taxable in that bracket rather than as personal income.

For Bogart's next picture, *The Barefoot Contessa*, his company received a percentage of the profits and he was paid a salary as well. *Contessa* was directed by Joseph L. Mankiewicz, the writer-director who once put Bogart down with his Oscars. Although Bogart was tired after *Sabrina* he wanted very much to work with Mankiewicz, and he thought the screenplay was excellent.

"In a nutshell, the plot is that life louses up the script," he told me. "In other words, it isn't always true that Cinderella meets Prince Charming and lives happily ever after. In this case Cinderella meets Prince Charming, but Prince Charming has been in a war and has been seriously damaged below decks. That's what the story is about."

The title, *The Barefoot Contessa*, was explained in a scene in which the Contessa, Ava Gardner, tells Bogart, playing a veteran Hollywood director and reformed drunk, about her childhood during the war in Spain. She was terrified of bombs and thought the earth was the safest place to be, and still feels more secure with her bare feet on the earth.

"She spends her evenings with whom she pleases," explains Bogie, "but her family always knew where to find her because when she visits a man she leaves her shoes outside his door."

The story by Mr. Mankiewicz very thinly resembled Rita Hayworth's life (the heroine is a beautiful Spanish dancer who becomes a star) and Bogart's role was, he said, "modeled after most of my friends who are ex-drunks." Marius Goring played a character very much like Aly Khan, and Edmond O'Brien played a Johnny Meyer-type press agent, a man long associated with Howard Hughes. A character resembling Hughes was played by Warren Stevens. "The whole thing is very adult, very exciting," said Bogart, who was so enthusiastic about the film that one might have thought it was his first big break.

Bogart was scheduled to arrive in Rome for the film just after New Year's, 1954. His Hollywood press agent, the late Bill Blowitz, who was one of the brightest publicity men in the film business, wired David Hanna, who was handling the picture: "Bogart arriving late Sunday night from New York. Don't photograph him without his hairpiece."

Hanna, an old pro in publicity, knew that it would be difficult to persuade Rome's reporters to cover Bogart's arrival on a Sunday night. So he marshaled all the publicity department's photographers, even the lab men, into service: a press-agent trick to impress a client.

The crowd met the plane with a flattering fuss. When the arrival formalities were concluded and Bogie and Hanna were in a car on the way to the hotel, Bogie lit a cigarette and, in recognition of the phony crowd, said to Hanna, "You don't have to bullshit an old bullshit artist like me. I know there's not much interest in my puss. I've been around long enough. We'll do a few stunts just to keep my name in the paper. I like publicity; it's good for an actor. But, let's face it, all the interest is going to be in Ava Gardner. She's the news, not me."

While working Bogart wouldn't touch a drop except at lunch until 6 o'clock, when, according to his contract, he was through for the day. Then, on the threshold of his portable dressing room, he would shout, "Scotch!" and his hairdresser would prepare drinks for himself and his companions.

Bogart's life away from Hollywood hardly varied when he was abroad. He ignored Italian food, claiming that he couldn't stand spaghetti, and so for two months had to live on Scotch and soup. He spent the evenings at an American restaurant near his hotel, the Excelsior, where he would gather with Edmond O'Brien, Joe Mankiewicz, Hanna, and others of the cast.

"This is my recreation," Bogie told Hanna, pointing to his whiskey. "I like to sit around and gab, enjoy my drinks and my family. That's what a man wants when he's over fifty! Drink never caused me any harm. Nobody can say it ever made me a poor husband. Unlike other pious slobs I've been faithful to all my wives. I like it that way, and I think I'm a damned good father."

Hanna said he was chagrined to discover that Bogie was not, at least at this time, living up to his reputation as a drinker. He invariably ordered English gin, considerably weaker than American. "And no man could murder a Scotch so unmercifully with water," Hanna said. "Moreover, he drank very slowly; so slowly that it often embarrassed me when I'd order two to his one."

One night Edmond O'Brien was in the depths of despair as he, Bogie, and Hanna sat in the hotel bar. O'Brien had fought a losing battle with his memory during an entire shooting day, trying to deliver a long telephone monologue.

"Don't be a chump," said Bogie, cigarette smoke curling around his thin lips, a glass of Scotch and water in his hands. "To hell with the lines. Stop worrying about them. That's not what the director wants. He wants that fat, pudgy face of yours; the sweat, the excitement a good actor like you knows how to generate. The woods are full of actors who can memorize a long speech. But can they play it?"

Then he told a story about how the director of a play, fed up with John Barrymore's inability to remember lines, fired him. He hired another actor who went through the part letter-perfect but made absolutely no impression on the audience. The manager had to beg Barrymore to come back.

Fortified by Bogie's confidence in him and by several Scotches, Eddie calmed down and went to the studio the next day where he tossed off the difficult scene in a couple of takes. The morning's work helped earn him an Academy Award for his role in *Contessa*.

"I'm not quite sure whether Bogie made up the Barrymore story or not," said Hanna. "I doubt that it fooled Eddie. But Bogie was intuitive about recognizing other people's need of reassurance—just as he required it himself."

Bogie didn't like Ava Gardner, his costar, and made no attempt to conceal it. He complained that as an actress she gave him nothing to work with. Consequently, when he felt a scene between them was going poorly he'd deliberately muff his lines in order to get a retake. His judgment was usually correct, and he deserved some of the credit Ava got for her performance.

Bogie refused to attend the premiere of *Contessa*. "Who the hell wants to see me drive up in a limousine and go into a movie house?" he asked Blowitz, his press agent. "Let Joan Crawford do it."

Bogart's next film was *We're No Angels*, a comedy based on a Broadway play about three convicts who are moved by the troubles of the family they meant to rob and end up playing Santa Claus. Peter Ustinov, one of the three convicts, was much impressed with Bogart. "His great basic quality," said Ustinov, "was a splendid roughness. Even when perfectly groomed I felt I could have lit a match on his jaw. He knew his job inside out, and yet it was impossible not to feel that his real soul was elsewhere, a mysterious, searching instrument knocking at doors unknown even to himself."

Bogart was in full presence on the set, however. "He carried the light of battle in his eyes," Ustinov said. "He wished to be matched, to be challenged, to be teased. I could see a jocular and quarrelsome eye starring out of the character he was playing into the character I was playing—rather as an experienced bullfighter might stare a hotheaded bull into precipitate action."

Unfortunately, the completed picture revealed little of the poetic fire described by Mr. Ustinov—the critics were only lukewarm to the picture and the performances.

Bogart started to search for a property of his own that would give him the kind of role he could relish.

"He was one of the few performers whose story judgment I could trust," Mary Baker told me. "He didn't care how big his part was but how good. When he wanted to do something he did it.

"He called me one day and said, 'Buy *Desperate Hours* for me. I want it.'

"The show was then a big hit on Broadway. I warned him that it was not going to be easy to buy and it might cost more than he wanted to spend.

" 'I'll authorize you to spend a quarter of a million dollars for it,' he said.

"I called New York, then called Bogie back and told him that wasn't enough money. He told me to go to $350,000.

"I did, but lost the movie to Paramount, which wanted it for William Wyler to direct. When I got back from lunch later that day I found Bogie in my lavatory peeing—the door open. He was absolutely blind drunk. I asked him what he was doing in my office.

" 'I want to talk to you,' he said. 'I might as well tell you, though, that you'll be unhappy. I've just been to lunch with William Wyler. We got drunk together and I committed myself to play in *Desperate Hours*. If I couldn't buy the story myself at least I can play in it.' "

Although Bogart had made a bad deal for himself financially and he knew it, he didn't care. "I would have paid

Willy to let me do it," he told Mary Baker when the picture was finished. "It was the best part I've had since *Petrified Forest*."

After *The Desperate Hours* Bogart went to Twentieth Century-Fox to make *The Left Hand of God* with Edward Dmytryk, who had directed him in *The Caine Mutiny*. "It was a nice little picture," Bogart told me once. "Nothing exciting, but nice."

Then Jerry Wald, who had produced many of Bogart's early pictures at Warner's, called to tell him about a prize-fight film he planned to make called *The Harder They Fall*. "It'll be a raw, realistic film about the fight racket," said Wald. Bogart was intrigued, but disgruntled when he heard that Wald planned to use several Broadway Method actors in lesser roles, including Rod Steiger, who was to be his co-star.

Although he accepted the role, he was fed up after a few days on the set working with Steiger, who believed in doing push-ups before a dramatic scene and walked around the set during lunch breaks murmuring his lines to himself and charging himself up for the scene to follow lunch. Bogart worked entirely differently; he completely relaxed at lunchtime, gave interviews, had his martinis, and then stepped into a scene refreshed and letter-perfect.

One morning Bogart telephoned Wald from the set. "I want to see you," he said. "Important?" asked Wald. "Of course," said Bogart.

Wald rushed over to Bogart's on-set dressing room. "I can't work with Steiger," Bogart said. "These Actors Studio types—they mumble their lines. I can't hear their words. I miss the cues. Why the hell don't they learn to speak properly. Words are important. This scratch-your-ass-and-mumble school of acting doesn't please me. You have to do something."

Wald pointed out that Steiger was a good actor. "I know he's good," said Bogart. "I like to see him on the screen. I just don't like working with him."

Tactfully, compromises were made in the production and direction and the picture moved on, though Bogart never let up on the Actors Studio types imported by Wald from Broadway. There were six or seven of them, none of whom except for Steiger had ever been in a film before, and Bogart never missed a chance to needle them.

Every time he gave an interview on set he would look to

see if one of them was near. If so, he would commence a diatribe about Method actors just to watch his barbs hit home.

It soon got to be a running gag among the Method actors because Bogart never said a word directly to any of them. On set one would ask the other if Bogie had spoken to him yet. "Well, he cleared his throat as he went by," one might answer with mock pride.

Mike Laine, a seven-foot-tall young man who played a simpleminded giant finagled into becoming a fighter by a ruthless promoter (Steiger) and an unemployed sportswriter (Bogart) was particularly aware of the silent treatment. One day toward the end of the film Bob Yeager, the publicity man, asked Mike if Bogie had spoken to him yet. "Once," said Laine. "You know the scene in the cab where Bogie and I are together? Well, Bogie jumped into the cab and said to me, 'Move over, kid.'"

Bogart was in top form during the picture. Between takes he and Bob Schiffler played backgammon. "He was a lousy player," said Schiffler. "He used to get fifty dollars a week allowance from his business manager, Morgan Maree. I would nurse him along for the first few days of each week. Then, about Thursday, he'd have to endorse the check over to me. One Thursday, after losing for the third straight week in a row, he got so furious that he threw the board in the air and belted me on the chin, knocking me ass over tea kettle. The next day I wore a boxer's helmet to work. When I walked in with it, he broke up laughing."

Some of the extras and featured players in the film actually were small-time fighters. One day one of them came up to Bogie's backgammon game and said, "Mr. Bogart, I'd like to ask your advice. It's so nice to be an actor, it's such a wonderful life, much better than fighting. I wonder if I shouldn't try to be an actor. What do you think?"

Bogart looked up from the game for a second, studied the man, then said, "I'll be brief. The answer is no."

Yeager recalled a day during filming when Darryl F. Zanuck gave an interview to a film trade paper saying there should be a search for fresh talent to hypo the business. "I was chatting with Bogie on the set, and mentioned the article to him. 'Guys like you are obsolete,' I told Bogie.

"'The hell we are,' said Bogie, pricked in the underbelly of his ego. 'What they want are new Bogarts, Gables, Coopers, and Stewarts—at seventy-five dollars a week!'

" 'Bogie, you could pull one of the best gags this town has ever seen,' I said.

" 'Take out a full-page ad in *Variety* to satirize new faces and new names. Get some old-time faces, yours included, and dress them up like Marlon or Tony Curtis or Rock Hudson and give them names like Spike or Nail. You could have a lot of fun.'

"When I had an idea Bogie always reacted strongly—he either chased me off the set with a baseball bat or immediately accepted it. This time he said, 'All right, you get the outfits and we'll do the picture.'

"We posed the picture that afternoon—Bogie in a torn sweatshirt, Max Baer in a suit with a huge bow tie, and Jersey Joe Walcott with a leather hat and sweater. The caption read: 'Spike Baer, Nails Bogart, Tack Walcott. The Oldest Established Permanent New Faces Now Available.'

"Then the studio wouldn't go for the four hundred and fifty dollars it cost. Wald, the producer, had liked the ad but he wanted to clutter it up with 'Jerry Wald Production in Panavision' with all the credits.

" 'He's screwing it up,' said Bogie. 'I am going to call him up, and you stay with me.'

"I never knew when Bogie was leading me over the leaves to the elephant trap but I had no choice. Bogie called Jerry, told him that he was spoiling the ad, then added, 'And Yeager is standing right next to me and he agrees.'

"There was the elephant trap and me on the stakes below. When Bogie hung up I asked him if he had to say that I was standing next to him; after all, I could be fired but they needed him. 'Why not?' Bogie said. 'If he says anything you tell me and I'll say it was my idea.' "

The ad was a big success. "Hollywoodites nearly swallowed their coffee cups this morning when they saw Movietown's funniest gag in years—a poke at Hollywood's 'new faces' campaign by that salty character, Humphrey Bogart," wrote the United Press's Aline Mosby.

Miss Mosby, who had found Bogart getting a haircut at the studio, reported that in "his informal and censorable language" he described why he declared war on the "new faces" search.

"New faces," he snorted. "Why don't they lift the old faces? The studios are full of hot air. Every couple of years studio heads say this. If they're going to make new stars, why haven't they made them by now? Brando and Jimmy Dean weren't made stars by studios. Studios can't make stars. After Miss Monroe left Fox they made some 'new star' as a substitute, but her name escapes me."

Bogart didn't forget to take a dig at the Method actors, either. "Those Tabs and Lances are gone in four or five years," he said. "And those new actors from New York . . . they scratch themselves in various places. They're trying to be what they call natural."

Bogart delighted in the furor the ad caused. And he was delighted about this time by something even more concrete. He was able to sell Santana Productions for more than a million dollars. The tax was only $250,000 since it was a capital gain, which meant he had a large sum of money intact for "Betty and the kids."

"An actor lives in a world of anxiety and insecurity," Bogie said. "He can't spread his big-money years over a lifetime like a businessman, he has to grab the bundle while he can. It's his only defense."

When the check came to Morgan Maree's office as all Bogie's checks did, Bogie was on hand to tell Morgan, "This is the one check I want to hold and look at for a few days."

"I don't blame him at all," said Maree.

Bogie had the check photostated and hung it on the wall of his den "to have something nice to look at." "It's a helluva lot prettier and more impressive to me than a painting worth seven hundred and fifty thousand dollars," he said.

One afternoon he took the framed copy of the check to lunch at Romanoff's and called over Sol Siegel, who had been slated to be his partner in Santana but accepted a job as MGM production head instead. With childish delight he jeered, "See what you missed."

TEN

The Harder They Fall was the last film Humphrey Bogart was to make. On the day before Christmas, 1956, when Bogie came on the set he was told he didn't have to work and could go home. "I wondered if he was going to say anything about Christmas," said Bob Yeager.

"He got to the stage door and halfway through it said, 'I'll see you all Monday.' He nearly closed the door, then opened it again and reluctantly said, 'Merry Christmas.' He was Scrooge right out of Dickens—but he said it."

Between Christmas and New Year's, 1956, Bogie had a bad coughing spell while lunching at Romanoff's with Buddy Fogelson, Greer Garson's husband. When he also complained that he had pain when swallowing, Romanoff, who had commented before on Bogie's coughing spells, pointed out that Buddy was going to the Beverly Hills Clinic to see a dentist after lunch: "Why don't you go along and have a doctor examine your cough," he suggested.

Without an appointment Bogie went to the office of Dr. Maynard Brandsma, a specialist in malignacies of the lung and throat. The doctor heard Bogie's symptoms, put him on a diet, and told him to cut down on smoking and drinking. Bogie laughed and said he'd see what he could do.

"Come back in three weeks," Dr. Brandsma said.

Three weeks later Bogie returned, complaining of the same pain.

"Did you stay on the diet?" the doctor asked.

"No," said Bogie.

"I can't help without your cooperation," the doctor said,

149

but now arranged to have Bogie's chest and esophagus X-rayed. Nothing showed up. Brandsma asked him to stick to the diet this time and report again in a few weeks.

Meanwhile Bogie and Betty were planning to make a movie together, *Melville Goodwin, U.S.A.* They had already done the wardrobe tests and signed the contracts. Although Bogart was not terribly concerned about the pain in his throat it continued to get worse so he went back to see the doctor.

This time Dr. Brandsma arranged to have Bogie bring in some of the mucus he coughed up in the morning during his coughing spells, which sometimes lasted as long as thirty minutes. The mucus was sent to the laboratory to be checked for malignant cells. The lab man reported that three of the five criteria for cancer were positive.

Another specimen, sent to the lab a week later showed that four of the five criteria were positive. Dr. Brandsma called Bogie into his office and told him he didn't know what was going on in his esophagus but recommended he be fluoroscoped. Bogie went to Good Samaritan Hospital in Los Angeles, where Dr. Michael Flynn found an ulcer immediately. He performed a biopsy. It was cancerous.

Dr. Brandsma told Bogie he had a malignant ulcer in the esophagus and would have to be operated on. "It's small and early enough in the game so I think we have time to get it," the doctor said.

"Can't we make the movie first, then the operation?" asked Bogie, who was scheduled to go before the cameras the following Monday.

"You can make the movie first—and you'll be a big hero at Forest Lawn," said Dr. Brandsma.

On a Friday morning in March Bogie called Mary Baker to say he had just come from the clinic and that he had a polyp on the esophagus that was supposed to be malignant. He had to have it taken out. Would Mary please call Milton Sperling, producer of the picture, and tell him it would have to be postponed a few weeks?

Dr. John Jones, a prominent Los Angeles surgeon, removed the ulcer but found, when he cut into the chest, that the cancer had spread to the lymph glands. They too were removed.

"I told Bogie that he had all the cancer out which we hoped was true," Dr. Brandsma said later. "In cancer you never know. He was in great pain, though, and he smoked like a chimney, so he had chemical bronchitis plus that terrible cough. Once, while in the hospital, his coughing ruptured all his stitches."

When he got home Bogie was not reluctant to admit he had been operated on for cancer. "Hell, I was in the operating room eight hours: I knew it wasn't tonsillitis," he told me. "Anyway, why shouldn't I say I had cancer. It's a respectable disease. It's nothing to be ashamed of. It's no worse than gallstones or appendicitis. They'll all kill you, if you don't do something about them soon enough."

Bogie was fascinated by the details of his operation. One afternoon when Dr. Brandsma came for a visit he had the doctor draw a complete diagram of the operation for Adolph Green who had dropped in.

Raymond Massey, who had come to Hollywood at the time to do a television show, was another guest taken along the gory route. Mr. Massey told me he went to visit Bogie armed with a fund of small talk and reminiscences, hoping to cheer him up. "I didn't know what to expect when I was ushered into the sick room, but there was Bogart, sitting in a chair, looking as good as ever, sipping a Scotch and soda, waiting for me. I was just beginning on the small talk when he cut in, 'I'll tell you what happened to me down there,' he said. 'It was awful!'"

Bogie went into great detail about the operation. "The sicker I got from his story the healthier he became," said Mr. Massey. "Then we spent a marvelous afternoon reminiscing about our adventures together."

Another who got the grisly treatment was Swifty Lazar, who brought a date to the house. "Spencer Tracy was there, too," said Swifty. "Both of them knew I can't stand talk about operations so they started to discuss them. I went into the other room at once which delighted them, but the girl stayed. She was fascinated but getting greener and greener as they made the stories gorier and gorier. Finally she went over in a dead faint. Bogie couldn't have been happier."

By June Bogie was aware that it was going to be a long fight. Alistair Cooke remembers going to see him on a day when Bogie was signing his will. "He spoke of it and of his illness and the sudden uselessness of money with an entirely unforced humor and an equally unforced seriousness: neither with complaint nor with a too-brave absence of complaint."

Although frequently in pain, Bogie refused to admit to it or give in to it, although he made some concessions. Clutching and shifting his four-speed Jaguar now tired him, so he traded it in on a Ford Thunderbird.

Five days before the end, Bogie was still entertaining guests downstairs at cocktail hour. It was a chilly January day and he was sitting in his old chair when I came in. A roaring fire was in the fireplace. On the table near him was a copy of _Compulsion_, the novel about the Loeb-Leopold murder case, and a bottle of Scotch. He was holding a martini in one hand and a cigarette with a long ash in the other. He was wearing a dressing gown and pajamas.

David Niven, still in makeup from a TV western, had dropped by after work to show Bogie a letter he had received from Douglas Fairbanks, Jr. Someone—I think it was Katie Hepburn—admired a new portrait that Claire Trevor had painted of Betty and Leslie for a Christmas gift. Betty said she liked it but thought her nose and mouth needed some repainting.

"That's the trouble with you actresses," needled Bogart. "You want all your pictures to be glamorous."

He wouldn't even admit to Dr. Brandsma how uncomfortable he felt, Dr. Brandsma told me. "I would come in to see him and ask how it was going. 'Rough,' he'd answer. 'Pretty rough?' I would ask. 'Yeah, pretty rough,' he'd answer.

"When a man is sick you get to know him. You find out whether he is made of soft or hard wood. I began to get fonder of Bogie with each visit: He was made of very hard wood indeed."

By mid-September Dr. Brandsma was aware that Bogie was not getting better—he was losing weight steadily—so he suggested X-ray treatments, a million volts a day for eight weeks.

The first time Bogie went into the X-ray room he was frightened—not at what the room was, because it was only a small room with white plaster walls, a tiny window, and the big X-ray machine suspended from the ceiling. He was frightened at what the room represented, he admitted to Betty. He had heard stories that it was the last resort in cancer treatment. He was completely alone, stripped to the waist and lying on the table with the cone onimously pointed like a Buck Rogers disintegrator gun at his stomach.

Behind the plaster were thick walls of lead. He was aware of the thickness because there was only one narrow window in the wall with a sheet of glass that looked to be a foot thick. Behind the window sat the technician who controlled the machine.

When the big cone descended from the ceiling and pin-pointed over his stomach there was no sound. He was given over to the machine. His sick body wasn't his any longer. It was divorced from his mind which was well.

After the first treatment he felt sick to his stomach. Later in the day, however, he felt a little better; the pain seemed to have diminished. And Dr. Brandsma was encouraging. He said they were making progress.

So he accepted the treatments, and for a while it appeared as though he was holding his own. "I'm going to beat it," he told Swifty enthusiastically after the first week of treatment. "I feel in my heart I'm going to make it."

ELEVEN

The *Santana*, a sleek 55-foot sailing yacht, was Bogie's therapy. He loved sailing and was as proud of his skill on the sea as his skill on the sound stage. On the boat he wanted to be thought of only as a sailor, not as an actor who dipped into sailing because he could afford it. And he was accepted by the sophisticated sailing fraternity as a sailor because of his excellence at the helm.

I asked him once why he loved sailing so much. "An actor needs something to stabilize his personality, something to nail down what he really is, not what he is currently pretending to be," Bogie said. Though he loved sailing very much, he thought of himself as an actor who sailed rather than as a sailor who acted.

Whether he had a good part coming up or whether the critics liked his picture never mattered on the ocean, which was one of the few places where he could get away from Hollywood and acting.

His life on the boat was divorced from his life in Hollywood. The only Rat Packers who went on the *Santana* regularly were David and Hjordis Niven, who loved sailing as he did. The others were more like Frank Sinatra, whose idea of a cruise to Catalina was to hire a power yacht with a band for dancing, broads for action, and lots of Jack Daniel's.

Sinatra was fun, however, and Bogie liked that. One of his favorite boating stories was of the time after he finished playing Captain Queeg in *The Caine Mutiny* and went on the *Santana* to forget the role. When they hit the first wave the boat was full of little steel balls rolling everywhere, tumbling from every nook and cranny on the ship. Sinatra had gone out a day earlier and hidden hundreds of ball bearings all over the boat as a gag. "I could have killed Frankie at first," Bogie said. "But it was a helluva gag."

Bogie frequently used the boat as a testing ground for people. If he didn't like someone, he would take him out on the boat with him for a day to find out why. Bogie believed that in the confinement of the *Santana*—with work to be shared—a man's character became apparent, just as it did when he was drunk.

Betty's farewell to the *Santana* came after an Ensenada race (which Bogie won) in which she was aboard as a passenger, cook, and barkeep. "I was below decks with the food all the time," she told me. "I must have been mad to do it."

I went with Bogie occasionally, usually with my own son who was Stephen's age. It was tacitly understood that since I was useless as a deckhand I was to function as baby-sitter and lifeguard, keeping the boys from falling into the water.

Stephen loved to sail with his father, and Bogie liked having him aboard. His dream was that one day Stephen would have as much respect and affection for the sea as he had. Bogie was training his son as his own father had trained him at the same age.

Stephen was aboard on Bogie's last sail. It was a bright day with the sun beating down on the Pacific. In the galley forward of the mainmast the rugged-looking Danish sailor-caretaker of the *Santana* who answered to the names of BS Pete (to the ladies) and Bullshit Pete (to the men) was hefting a case of Scotch while the boy scampered around the mahogany deck, shrieking with delight. "When you're all secure up forward, the skipper would like a little liquid refreshment," called out Bogie from the cockpit, unshaven and clothed in a duffle coat and black peaked yachting cap with the Los Angeles Yacht Club insignia.

"Coming right up, Mr. Bogart," shouted Pete, who poured from a freshly opened bottle two shot glasses of Scotch. He came aft to the hatchway and handed up one of the glasses.

"To the weather," he said, hoisting the glass to his lips and draining it.

Bogie sipped his whiskey more thoughtfully. "You'll finish the bottle before we get under way, you old drunk," he said, a grin slicing the edge off his words.

"We'll get under way whenever you say, Mr. Bogart," said Pete.

"I say now," said Bogie. "Keep an eye on Steve, will you. His mother would never forgive me if I came home . . ."

A coughing spasm interrupted the sentence. Pete turned away, pretending not to notice it, and busied himself with preparations for casting off, which included lacing the protesting boy into a life jacket.

With the *Santana* under way and heeled over at a precarious angle Pete trimmed the jib. Bogie sat at the wheel, an unlit cigarette in his mouth, his narrowed eyes glancing restlessly from the compass to the billowing mainsail and jenny.

Bogie looked off to port. A larger boat had taken the same tack and was racing along next to him. He glanced at Pete, who gave the mainsail an extra hitch.

"Just like the Channel Island race, Skipper," Pete said and told me of the day the Coast Guard called to ask if the *Santana* was able to stand a fifty-six-mile-an-hour wind. "Well, we're doing it aren't we?" Bogie replied. "We passed the *Morningstar* hove to, and the *Cubasco,* which was 10 feet longer," said Pete proudly. "We passed them all and made it to port."

For the fourth year in succession Bogie won the race and retired the cup. It was on the mantel next to his Oscar—"The only two awards I really cherish," he once told me.

The *Santana* began to pull away from the other boat. The exhilaration when he was in a race—whether winning or not, just being in the race—pumped color into Bogie's cheeks.

He sat huddled in the duffle coat handling the helm and leaving us to our own thoughts. Beyond the spray that the sharp bow was tossing up into the sun I could see in my mind's eye those familiar banks of studio lights and the hairy men who handle them and theaters on opening nights with the sidewalks roped off to keep back pressing crowds. Even more clearly I saw Bogie in his best roles: Sam Spade giving up the girl because he knew he'd never be able to trust her; the broken-down bum on the Tampico park bench holding forth on his favorite subject: that gold need not change men; Duke Mantee with a tommy gun across his knees confronting the effete Englishman and the plump girl behind the counter.

Forward, Pete said to Carl, the cook, "He's never happier than when he's in a race." Pete watched the skipper for a minute. "Christ. Nobody ever loved a woman the way he loves this boat."

"How much longer do we have to go, Daddy?" Stephen asked his father in a small voice.

"You frightened?" Bogie asked. "We're going to Balboa, right up there about a mile further. You'll like it, Steve. We'll anchor and loaf and you'll fish with Pete."

While the *Santana* lay at a mooring at the Newport Harbor Yacht Club, the boy and Pete fished and Bogie sat in the cockpit with newspapers, magazines, books, binoculars, cigarettes, and Scotch, reading, looking, and thinking. He ate very little —a dollar-sized pancake and a piece of dry toast was all he could force down. Although a bottle was always at his elbow, he drank little. He refused to go ashore.

On the first evening Pete went to the Clubhouse to check in. Victor McLaglen saw him and said, "Let's have the old bastard in for a drink."

"I don't think Mr. Bogart feels well," said Pete.

"He's fifteen years younger than I am, he should feel well. Tell him to come in and have a drink on me."

Pete returned to the mooring and relayed the message. "Tell him to leave me alone," snapped Bogie. "I just want to sit here in the cockpit."

Milton Bren and Claire Trevor came down to visit. Claire and Bogie had been close friends for years and had appeared in many pictures together. He looked so ill that in a motherly gesture, she stroked him on the arm.

"Leave me alone and get off my boat," he snapped. "I don't want any sympathy."

When they left he said he was sorry he had spoken so harshly. After all they were old friends. But dammit, he didn't want sympathy—theirs or anyone else's. "Milton will understand," he said.

A dinghy passed nearby, powered by an outboard motor. Two men in bathing suits were drinking beer out of cans. One of them hailed the *Santana*.

"Going out for a sail, Bogie?"

Bogie cupped his hands to his mouth. "Sure, going up to the beach," he called. Although he tried to yell they couldn't hear him. He waved them away with a forced smile.

"Who's that?" asked Stephen, who had just come back.

"Some friends of mine. You with the F.B.I. or something?"

"I just wondered," said the boy.

Reaching for his son, Bogie pulled him down next to him in the cockpit.

"In a couple of years," he said, "you'll be coming with me every weekend. No more hanging around the house. I started sailing when I was your age. There's nothing better for a man."

He started to cough, his body bent forward with pain as the force of the cough tore at him. The boy, uncomfortable, seized the excuse to go forward, where Carl was scaling and preparing the fish for dinner.

While the boy was gone Bogie sat at the helm with Pete talking about some of the crazy things that had happened to them in the past, like the night in '56 when Pete took a young friend of Bogie's in the skiff to pick up Bogie at the Yacht Club. As they went by a big pink house on the Isthmus they were hailed by a man who told them that Roy Rogers' skipper had just been shot through the arm by an unknown sniper. Would they help search the boats at the dock?

Pete and the boy joined a search party but the sniper was not found. As they left the group to go get Bogie, a bullet whistled by Pete's ear. Pete ducked down and another bullet whistled over his head and hit the boy in the rump. Pete rowed the young man back to the big pink house and helped carry him into the den, where he was laid alongside Rogers' wounded skipper waiting for the doctor. Pete said he had to get his boss and would come right back to Rogers with him.

When he got to the Yacht Club Bogie was on the landing waiting for him. "For Chrissake, Pete, where you been? You're twenty-five minutes late," Bogie said.

"I know. I'm sorry. I been shot at."

"I can see you're half shot already," said Bogie. "Where's the kid?"

"He's laying on the floor over there shot," said Pete, gesturing toward the pink house.

"You mean you got the kid drunk already?" asked Bogie.

"No, sir, he just got shot and I been shot at. Right by my ear."

"Pete, are you shitting me?" asked Bogie.

"No, sir."

"Where is he?"

"In the pink house over there."

Bogie hustled into the skiff and helped Pete row over to the house where the kid was lying on the floor moaning with pain.

Bogie ignored everyone in the room and angrily asked if anyone wasn't going to give the kid a drink. When no one answered he said, "Pete, go pour the kid a drink."

When the doctor came Bogie said he would guarantee the boy's medical bills. He helped carry the kid to the ambulance, then walked back to the skiff with Pete, who said, "You know, Mr. Bogart, that man in the house was Roy Rogers."

"Roy who?" asked Bogie.

"The cowboy actor. Roy Rogers."

"You're kidding," said Bogie.

"No, I'm not. He had a gun belt on and boots and a hat. That was Roy Rogers."

Bogie recollected that the man was indeed wearing cowboy garb.

"You're right, Pete," he said. "Let's go back to the house."

When they went in Bogie apologized for having ignored Rogers. "I'm sorry I didn't recognize you," he said. "Let's have a drink."

"Sure," said Rogers, "but please don't say anything in the papers about all this."

"What papers?" asked Bogie.

"Well, ain't you a newspaperman?" said Rogers.

The mood of nostalgia was interrupted by the presence on the dock of the Club Commodore, Brett Fullmore. Pete ignored the commodore and went forward, leaving the commodore to stare with obvious distaste at the unshaven man in the cockpit of the *Santana*. Bogie stared back, eyes flat and expressionless.

The commodore made a move as if to come forward, but not receiving any encouragement from Bogie he turned back and walked slowly toward the club. Bogie was pleased. "That's a man who won't forget me," he said, and told for the umpteenth time of his last meeting with the commodore.

One day after sailing he and Pete went into the clubhouse for a drink. Fullmore came over, took Bogie aside, and said, "I'm sorry, Mr. Bogart, but it's a club rule that hired hands are not allowed at the bar."

"What do you mean, hired hands?" said Bogie angrily. "I don't have any hired hands. This is my friend, Pete."

"Well, he's working for you," said the commodore.

"The hell he is," said Bogie. "The SOB never did a goddam thing for me. He belongs to the Danish Royal Yacht Club and he's going to join the New York Yacht Club—Commodore Roosevelt told him to. In fact he has his application in here, too, but I'm going to withdraw it."

The commodore squirmed uncomfortably. Bogart, warming to the subject and happy at the commotion he was making, said, "If you want us to go, we'll go." Then he shouted, "Everybody come to the *Santana*. The drinks are free."

Within minutes the club was emptied. "It cost a case of Scotch to make my point but it was worth it," Bogie said.

In the galley Pete and the cook were arguing about dinner. Carl, the cook, was a part-time fireman, a fact Pete always mentioned when he criticized the cooking. Both men were obviously a little drunk.

"Everyone who has ever worked for me seems to end up as an alcoholic," Bogie said, and told me how he met Pete and how Pete came to work for him.

It was back in '49 when he was married to Mayo. He was sitting on the deck of their cruiser, *Sluggy*, when he noticed a yacht coming into port next to him. The captain brought her into the dock without a murmur of wood against wood and discharged his passengers, then using an outboard he backed her out, turned her around, and backed in again—a skillful feat of seamanship.

He called over a compliment to the captain, a rugged-looking man about his age. He invited him over for a drink, found his name was Pete, and after some amenities said, "Pete, someday I'm going to have a sailboat and I want you to work for me."

Later that night when Mayo and he were having their usual battle—bottles through windows, cursing, slapping, and screaming—Pete came over to see what the noise was about. "Can I help you, sir?" he asked.

"Why didn't you come before?" Bogie said. "I've got her down now."

She was down on the deck, blood all over her but "happy as she always was after she had forced me to lose my temper and hit her back," he remembered.

Pete came to work for Bogie after he had bought the *Santana* from Dick Powell for $50,000. First, he hired a skipper who was an alcoholic. One day Pete called to say the skipper had quit and he was taking over with Mr. Bogart's permission.

"I taught Pete he wasn't a sailor if he couldn't drink a quart a day," said Bogie. "I broke him in and taught him how—take the first one in the morning with coffee and two ounces an hour for the rest of the day."

Forward we heard the voices of the two men raised too loudly. "Always fighting, those two," said Bogie. "It's wonderful. They must really like each other or they couldn't fight so much." He told me of the night that Carl went after Pete with a knife. They had guests aboard—Commodore George Roosevelt, Phil Berg, and Milton and Claire Bren—and Bogie had warned Pete that he wanted him and the cook sober.

The two men had an argument in the galley about the way lobster should be served. Pete hit Carl, and the cook, knife in hand, chased him to the deck. He could still see them—the six-foot-two cook towering over Pete, holding him with one hand, the other with knife raised.

"Mr. Bogart, I can't get along with this man," said Pete in the understatement of the year.

Bogie went between the men. "Pete, you get forward where you belong," he bellowed. "Cook, you get into the galley. And I don't want to hear another word from either of you. God-dam it, that's an order."

From across the water we heard the sounds of a party on a yacht moored in the mist. The drunken laugh of a woman interrupted Bogie's reverie. "Floating motels and whore-houses, most of these boats," he said. "A boat's the best place in the world to shack up." Looking out from the cock-pit of the *Santana* he sighed. "The only woman I ever had aboard her was Betty," he said. "And that usually with dis-astrous results—like the time Pete quit because of Betty."

He laughed in the night, recalling the trip to Catalina he had conned Betty into. Pete had done himself proud as a sailor that time. They went over under sail in fog so thick that the first thing they saw in Catalina was their buoy. Betty sat in the stateroom cursing all the way the stupidity that had led her to make the trip.

The next morning at seven Pete as always went over the hull with a wet chamois. Then he shined the brass, leaving the winch over Betty's bunk until last. At eight he began to pol-ish the winch, making a tremendous whirr as the rag forced it to spin.

Betty leaped out of her bunk, furious at being awakened so early by such noise. She stuck her head through the hatch and shouted, "What are you doing, you son of a bitch?"

When he and Betty appeared on deck at noon, Pete was no-where to be seen. Betty made ham and eggs in the galley, then rowed off in the skiff to dump the garbage.

While she was gone Pete reappeared. "Where were you all morning?" Bogie asked.

"Oh," said Pete, "I quit this morning."

"You did what?"

"I quit."

"Why?"

"Didn't you hear what Mrs. Bogart said to me?"

"So what," Bogie said. "For Chrissake, if I can take it every day you can take it once a year."

Suddenly, from the cabin Pete appeared to ask if we were ready to chow down.

"Forget about chow," Bogie said. "Have Steve come up to say good-night. I'm going to stay out here."

Pete looked at his boss in dismay. "It's too cold, Mr. Bogart," he said.

"I want to stay out here," said Bogie firmly.

After Pete left Bogie pulled the hood of his duffle coat up over his cap and lit a cigarette. For years whenever he lit a cigarette he would say to me jokingly, "Another nail in the coffin."

He plunged his hands deeper into the duffle and settled comfortably against the varnished coaming of the cockpit. He slept and woke up in the morning with the smell of coffee in his nostrils.

"Didn't want to wake you but the gang is due," Pete said. "My head. It aches."

"Of course, it aches, you Danish bastard," Bogart snarled. "You drank up all my Scotch."

"That's what it's there for, ain't it?" countered Pete.

"For me to drink, not you," he said.

At eight-thirty the gang began to arrive—Bob, Jeff, the Goon—others. And the routine was as always. After the exchange of friendly insults Bogie carefully supervised Pete's provisioning of the *Santana*'s galley and liquor locker for a day afloat: several brands of beer for those who preferred it, and a nice box full of iced crab and lobster.

Bogie, favoring his sore back, sat by the helm, binoculars in hand, studying the other craft and calling out comments to Pete.

By nine the crew was aboard and the sails unfurled. The *Santana* caught the wind and sailed majestically out beyond the Long Beach breakwater. Bogart sniffed the sea air, and waved hello to the Pacific.

The *Santana* heeled over onto a direct course to Catalina and by lunchtime we were moored at White's Landing. Bogie called it "The Gold Coast" because so many millionaires had their yachts moored there. The boating fraternity waved, and Bogie and crew waved back.

Pete began to serve up the lobster and crab, cracked and chilled. "This is the reward I've been waiting for," said Schiffler, wet and cold under his slicker like the rest of us.

There was talk at lunch about Bogie's shakedown cruise on the *Santana* in 1946, just over a decade before.

His dream always had been to own a sailing yacht and when he heard Dick Powell was going to sell the *Santana* he decided that no matter what the cost he would have her. The *Santana* was to the yachting fraternity what Whirlaway was to racetrack boys. She came in second to *Dorade* in the Santa Monica-Honolulu race in 1934 and was the pride of the Pacific Coast.

After Bogart bought the boat Powell agreed to check him out on her in a shakedown cruise. But Bogie couldn't wait: He bundled Betty into the car and went down the night before so they could sleep on her and he could admire the sleekness and beauty of her lines. He even brought a can of brass polish for the brightwork (which was unnecessary since every inch of her was polished and gleamed). Early in the morning Powell appeared out of the fog in his dinghy.

There was trouble getting the motor started and for an hour the old owner apologized to the new for the problem while they were down in the engine room cursing at the fuel pump.

Finally the engine got going and with Powell at the helm they ran out of the harbor and past the jetty. There was no wind and the haze was too great to see Catalina, but they decided to hoist the sails anyway so Bogie could find out where things were.

The amateur crew, friends of Powell's, went to work efficiently and within minutes she was dressed in full rigging. Although the sails were luffing they decided to go to Catalina under sail anyway.

At dusk, the rough outline of Catalina rose up out of the mist and they moored for the night in a quiet cove. Betty, who had been alternating between the helm and the galley, produced dinner and they listened to the radio afterward: It was the day that Tilden beat Stoefen and everyone cheered.

The next day they caught a good wind. The *Santana* heeled over and her lean bow split the waves into neat slices. Bogie was filled to bursting with the pride of ownership, and

Powell looked sad because he had loved her, too, and was parting with her.

Betty, looking at her husband's joyful face under the two-day growth of beard, said, "He's the ugliest handsome man I have ever seen."

But that was long ago. Since then he had added as much to the *Santana*'s luster as she added to his. He had won the four Channel Island races, and he'd earned the respect of the sailing fraternity up and down the Coast. Many of the old salts didn't even know he was an actor during his spare time. One character who accosted him on the wharf as he was tying up the *Santana* asked him what he did for a living. "I act in pictures," Bogie said. There was a long pause while the old fellow shifted the tobacco plug to the other side of his mouth. "Talkies?" he asked.

Although Doctor Brandsma had said Bogie was not to eat any spicy foods, smoke, or drink, he asked Carl to go ashore and buy the hottest chile he could find.

Schiffler looked at him with curiosity. "I just can't seem to put on any weight," Bogie explained, but Schiffler shrugged and went back to the cracked lobster.

Carl came back with the chile and we all piled into it. It was hot all right: It felt like a cargo of hot coals sliding down my gullet. It seared and burned and choked, but it felt solid.

"Damn doctor," Bogie said. "No wonder I don't gain weight; they don't give me the right kind of food to eat. I'll go on my own diet and show them."

Bob Millotte started to pour the drinks: Jeff Richards held out a coffee mug for his Scotch. The Goon, Schiffler's wife, started to mix him a martini.

"I'll have Scotch," Bogie said.

She looked at her husband, who nodded. "He's the skipper," Schiffler said.

"Damn well told," grumbled Bogie.

The conversation, as often happened at some time on a weekend like this, was about God: Sailors who live under the sky and on the vast ocean are never far from an awareness of the Deity. Jeff said something to the effect that "It was too bad that God made men in His image and then man tried to make God in his image."

It was a familiar polemic, but Bogie leaped into the argument with his old enthusiasm. Within minutes he had Jeff boiling mad at him. Then he turned to Bob and got him mad, and in a moment had them both mad at each other. He settled back in the cockpit happily.

"Damn it, Bogie's done it again," Jeff said to Bob. "When are we going to learn?"

Betty called on the ship-to-shore telephone. "Just wanted to say 'hello' to you, that's all, darling," she said. "Are you all right?"

"Fine," he said, "just fine. But I miss you."

"Let me talk to Bob," Betty asked.

Bob reassured her that Bogie was all right and handed the phone back. "See you Sunday at six," Bogie told her.

When Bogie hung up, Schiffler was midway through the story of the time the maître d' at the Balboa Yacht Club refused to allow him and Bogie to come in without a tie. "A tie is necessary, Mr. Bogart," the maître d' insisted. So Bogie and Bob went outside, removed their shirts, and came in naked to the waist—but with ties.

It was one of Bob's favorite stories when he was getting tipsy, and everyone had heard it before, but they all roared with laughter.

In the stern the gang was getting tipsier, and someone on another boat shone a light on them, shouting, "Quiet down on the *Santana*." The spotlighted party reminded Bogie of another scene that was spotlighted when he was married to Mary Philips, and he told us of it. He and Mary went to a party on the Hudson River in New York one night at Fay Bainter and Reginald Venable's home. Commander Venable had ordered his destroyer up the Hudson in front of his home and had her searchlights illuminate the grounds for the party. The tide went out, leaving the destroyer grounded. Commander Venable was court-martialed, but the party was a raging success.

The rest of that night and the next day passed in a pleasant haze of memories relived, jokes and insults and camaraderie.

At 4 P.M. we were back at the mooring and by five the *Santana* was swabbed bright and fresh, the sails furled and bagged, and Pete was tipsily waving good-bye from the cockpit.

Schiffler insisted on driving Bogie home through the freeway traffic, the Goon following in their car. It was six on the dot when he arrived, and Betty was waiting with a kiss and the warmth that all sailing men deserve when they return home from the sea.

TWELVE

The relief nurse was a big fellow, with a cheerful, competent air. He was carrying in his hand the file folder that had the charts on Bogie's progress and treatment.

Betty had seen the notes many times and reported, "There's nothing in them, Humphrey."

Bogie reached for the folder casually, saying, "Haven't seen it for a couple of days."

The nurse handed the charts over.

Bogie nonchalantly thumbed to the last page of the chart and studied it. The entry was noncommittal, merely showing a three-pound weight loss with the note, "No improvement." Casually he thumbed back to the first entry, then read forward. The notes showed a distinct trend: He was getting thinner and thinner. "No improvement."

When Dr. Brandsma got to Bogie's bedroom, his patient was waiting anxiously. "I don't seem to be getting any better, Doc," Bogie said. "I'm a little worried. Am I getting worse or is it what you expect?"

Betty, who was there at the time, told me that the question was asked so there was an out. "He didn't want a direct answer," Betty said.

And he didn't get one.

"Bogie, this is a long haul," the doctor said. "You can't expect these things to clear up right away. I think you're holding your own pretty well."

Bogie made no comment.

Durng the last month Bogie saw many of his old friends. "There was no strain of any kind, because (I believe) he knew the worst and was resolved to rouse himself for two hours a day to relax with his friends until the end came," Alistair Cooke wrote. "Another of his triumphant deceptions was that he managed to convince everybody that he was intermittently uncomfortable but not in pain.

"It is hard for actors to avoid the dramatizing of their emotional life, whether grossly by 'living the part' or subtly by sentimental deprecation. Bogart was merely himself, a brave man who had come to terms as we all may pray to do with the certain approach of death."

Adlai Stevenson, who also saw him in that last month, said, "He was very ill and very weak. But he made a most gallant effort to keep gay. He had an impatience for weakness, an impatience with illness."

Truman Capote visited him a few times. "He seemed to bring out the best in all of his friends," the writer said. "He looked so awful, so terribly thin. His eyes were huge and they looked so frightened. They got bigger and bigger. It was real fear and yet there was always that gay brave self."

Fourteen days before the end, Bogie was still hopeful he would get well. He asked Aurilio Salazar to take his Thunderbird down and have it serviced. "I'm going to take Stephen to Newport for a cruise again," he said. "I want the car ready."

Then he began to weaken quickly. "He went through the worst and most agonizing pain any human can take," Dr. Brandsma said. "I knew this, but he never complained, never whimpered. I knew he was dying and, during the last week, I knew he knew it by the questions he would ask."

During that last week Pete, skipper of the *Santana*, came by one afternoon for a visit. When Betty brought Pete into the bedroom Bogie asked hoarsely, "What the hell are you doing here?"

"I was just lonesome," said Pete.

"I knew it," said Bogie. "You don't care about me, you just want a drink. Go pour yourself one."

Pete went over to the portable bar in the bedroom and poured himself a Scotch and water.

"What's the matter with a drink for me?" demanded Bogie.

"Can you take one?" asked Pete.

"Goddam right I can. There's never a time when I can't take a drink with you."

Pete poured another Scotch and water and brought it to

Bogie, who reached out from the bed for the glass, saw the color, and demanded to know, "What the hell is that?"

"Scotch and water, like you asked for."

"You didn't ask me what I wanted. I'm drinking vodka and Schweppes. Leave it the way it is. It's beautiful, just as you are."

I noticed the copy of *Compulsion* on the table and mentioned it was the book Marie McDonald had been reading before she was kidnapped. Bogie asked me how I knew and I told him I had been covering the story all week. "Well, go on," he demanded impatiently. "Let's hear the facts you aren't writing for the *Herald Tribune*."

When Betty decided that Bogie had had enough company he tried to act irritated, but it was apparent that he was tired.

Friday morning Bogie telephoned Jess Morgan in Morgan Maree's office to say that some of the press had been writing stories that he was dying of cancer. "Get me a lawyer, I'm going to sue them," he said. Jess called Martin Gang, a prominent Hollywood attorney, and explained the situation. The two men went to see Bogie, who was in bed.

"Bogie's voice faded in and out toward the end of the conversation but he asked Martin to prepare a law suit," Morgan recalled. "He was full of fight even though he was obviously very sick."

Friday afternoon Mary Baker went to the house. After a short visit Bogie took her hand and squeezed it. He usually said, "See you tomorrow," but this time he said, "Good-bye, Mary."

Saturday morning Morgan Maree dropped by on his way to Northern California for some pheasant shooting. "I'll look in again when I get back Monday morning," he said. Bogie squeezed his old friend's hand, and said, "Okay, kid."

Saturday afternoon Swifty Lazar came by the house as usual. "I used to go every day to see him because he knew how I hated sickness and death and, if I missed a night, he'd say to Betty, 'Swifty thinks I'm going to die.'"

Saturday night Spencer Tracy and Katharine Hepburn were leaving just as Dr. Brandsma arrived. Miss Hepburn kissed Bogie good night as she always did. Tracy, who was standing behind Bogie, put his hand on his shoulder and leaned forward. "Bogie looked up at him with a most rueful smile, and said, 'Good-bye, Spence,' and you could tell he meant it," said Miss Hepburn. "He'd always said 'Good night' before. When we were downstairs, Spence looked at me, and said, 'Bogie's going to die.' "

When Dr. Brandsma finished his evening visit, Bogie said "Good-bye" to him and thanked him for everything he had done. The doctor told me, "I am sure that night he knew he was going to die."

After Dr. Brandsma left, Betty went to kiss Bogie good night. "I don't know why but that night I slept on the bed with him," Betty told me. "In the morning before I took the kids to Sunday School he woke up and said, "Boy, I hope I never have another night like that again." He never did.

When Betty came back to the house fifteen minutes later Bogie was in a coma and the nurse had phoned Dr. Brandsma, who rushed to the house.

At 2:10 on the morning of January 14, 1957, Bogie took his last gulp of life—a deep one.

Betty telephoned me at 2:30. She was sobbing, but her voice was firm. "Bogie died tonight, Joe," she said. "It was the last story he could give you and he wanted you to have it first."

THIRTEEN

Bogie died nine years ago, and although millions were momentarily saddened that this fascinating figure was gone, the world soon moved on to other matters, as it always does.

But then there appeared some signs that Bogart was not forgotten. Managers of arty movie houses noticed that Bogart revivals pulled good crowds—a double-bill of *The Big Sleep* and *To Have and Have Not* broke all attendance records at Manhattan's New Yorker Theater, for example. The Brattle Theater in Cambridge, Massachusetts, patronized largely by Harvard students, has for years successfuly scheduled a Bogart Film Festival during every exam period. *Time* pontificated that there was a Bogart cult: "Bogie worship is spreading."

Bogart cult or not, Bogie is proving to be the most durable movie personality in memory, far outlasting more celebrated matinee idols. In their heyday Clark Gable and Gary Cooper were considerably more popular, but their deaths did not bring their old movies back into vogue.

Meanwhile, on movie and television screens, Bogie's memory stays very much alive, both here and abroad. Lauren Bacall, now married to actor Jason Robards, still gets fan mail addressed to Bogart. "Lots of people just won't accept the fact that he's gone," she told me. Currently some five books are reportedly being written about him, and I wasn't surprised last summer to see in remote Dubrovnik, Yugoslavia, that the current attraction at the local movie house was *High Sierra*. It seems likely that in death Bogart has come close to his own rigorous test of fame. "You're not a star," he once told me, "until they can spell your name in Karachi."

What is it about Bogart that makes him such a durable figure? What charismatic qualities does he have that appeal to two generations, to matrons and hipsters, to co-eds and professors?

Part of the answer lies in his very real ability as an actor. As evidence, when Bogie did a role it tended to stay done. In a cannibalistic business where remakes of successful remakes are the rule, no actor today is foolhardy enough to try to play his roles in *The African Queen, The Maltese Falcon, The Petrified Forest* or the other great ones. And in terms of sheer footage, his accomplishment was prodigious. In his quarter of a century before the cameras he made seventy-five pictures, and no other film actor has ever had a higher percentage of hits, many of which became classics. No star today, when a movie may take a year or more to make, could ever hammer his image so compellingly into the public mind.

But far beyond his performance on the screen, the Bogart mystique today is based on the memory of his incandescent personality. As Lauren Bacall sees it, "His own character and integrity and honor permeated everything he did. Amid all the hysteria and madness of our world today there was in Bogie a thread of security and sanity that everyone respects. Audiences know that no matter what happened nobody could make him veer from the path he was on. He was always true to himself, his friends, and his family. Most important, he was his own man. I think that's what people want to identify with."

Certainly Bogie's masculinity and strength, even his toughness, represent something that many women—and men—are seeking today. In a world where homosexuality is becoming commonplace there are too few strong father images in life, let alone on the screen. Bogart still stands out above the current crop of leading men who are too handsome, too perfect, too cute. As the film industry reaches new technical heights the actors become paper dolls moved by directors, cameramen, and cutters, not by any inner fire.

In contrast, Bogart was an individual of great authority and strength, who bowed to no man or cop. He was completely self-reliant: Just try to imagine him on a psychiatrist's couch. On or off the screen, if he had a problem he solved it himself, whether wisely or not. He took on Fate single-handed.

Bogart was, as Alistair Cooke has said, a child of his chaotic times. He grew up in the turbulence and insecurity of the twenties and thirties—tough times that required tough men. He learned to rely on nothing but himself, and he was perhaps too proud of the fact that he never asked for anyone's help.

Another aspect of Bogart's enduring appeal was his unqualified honesty. Whether playing a gangster or a private eye he portrayed a man who unflinchingly followed his own code of ethics no matter how difficult or dangerous the road. Even now, long after his pictures were made, he still stands for strength and honesty in a world and in an industry where both are rare.

He was honest with his emotions, on screen and off. When he tenderly kisses Rosemary in *The African Queen*—one of the highlights of the film—you can see the real, unguarded Bogart. He was not afraid to expose his naked feelings to the camera or to his friends because he was not ashamed of them. When he talked of his love of Lauren Bacall there was no question in your mind of his sincerity, and he was one of those rare men who can cry, not out of frustration or self-pity, but from honest grief.

"His yes meant yes, his no meant no; he always said what he believed and backed up his beliefs; there was no bunkum about Bogart," Katharine Hepburn told me.

He resented bunkum even in small matters, such as wearing a toupee. He wanted to age before his public without faking or flinching, and I recall how angry he was when he had to wear a toupee in some films to look younger. He was humiliated by the artificiality and considered it effeminate.

Bogart, who didn't give a damn whether he was seen unshaven or untoupeed, made a career of his homeliness. He was what he seemed to be—an imperfect man, but a man. "His very homeliness is what made him attractive to women," suggested Andrew Sarris, editor of *Film Culture*. "There's an element of narcissism in most good-looking men. Homely men can escape themselves. They are not smug and complacent."

Just as Bogie's homeliness became an asset, his honesty about himself worked to his advantage. The happy reconciliation between private and public image was heavily exploited in the press, to the delight of a public that found in the

screen shadow the substance of the real man. As a result,
no amount of scandal could hurt him or his career. His
four marriages had no more adverse effects on his popularity
than his occasional nightclub battles or his fondness for
Scotch. These things were expected of him.

Bogart was a maverick off screen as well as on. He was a
fearless liberal at a time when most of his generation were
cowering silently under the threat of McCarthyism. Long
before most Americans acknowledged the tragic plight of the
Negro he spoke out in interviews against segregation and
prejudice, knowing full well that he would be bitterly criticized for airing such opinions.

In a community that worshiped money as power and status
he advised young actors to "take the big part but hold off on
the big house and the big car or you'll be in hock to the
studio the rest of your life." The only point in making money,
he said, was "so you can tell some big shot to go to hell."

Underneath this hard-boiled exterior there was an appealing purity, almost Victorian, which may contribute to his enduring magnetism. Although his conversation was strongly
spiced with profanity he was never salacious and he never
talked about sex. "I always suspect people who talk too much
about acting or sex," he once told me. "You either do it and
don't talk about it or you talk about it and don't do it."

There was a curious parallel between James Dean and Bogart. Both were masters of the "I don't give a damn" attitude. Both have had a lasting impact on young people, a
phenomenon all the more remarkable when one considers
that Dean was twenty-four when he died, and Bogie was fifty-
seven. But there was a basic difference between them.

I once brought Dean out to meet Bogie, who was impressed
with the younger man's talent but didn't like him. "He's too
conscious of himself every minute," Bogart said. He was right
—Dean was continually aware of the impression he was making, while Bogart was supremely self-confident. Whereas Dean
tried to impress the world by conforming to nonconformity,
Bogie adhered only to his own rules.

It is not surprising that Bogart was an admirer of Ernest
Hemingway, because the actor and the writer felt very
much alike on the kind of code that should govern a man's
life. The essence of that code is courage and style, and it
was with these two guidelines that Bogie faced his last illness. Katharine Hepburn told me she believed that he knew
he was dying but didn't wish to discuss it. "As long as he

didn't admit it he knew everybody had to play the game with him, and a very fine game it was," said Miss Hepburn. "It was the game of life. He was always willing to pay the price for anything he did. He thought he had had a great life, and he was willing to pay for it."

Bogie passed the final test of man with flying colors. Now he also seems to be passing the test of timelessness.

More Bestsellers from SIGNET

☐ **BRING ME A UNICORN: The Diaries and Letters of Anne Morrow Lindbergh (1922-1928) by Anne Morrow Lindbergh.** Imagine being loved by the most worshiped hero on Earth. This nationally acclaimed bestseller is the chronicle of just such a love. The hero was Charles Lindbergh; the woman he loved was Anne Morrow Lindbergh; and the story of their love was one of the greatest romances of our time. "Extraordinary . . . brings to intense life every moment as she lived it."—**New York Times Book Review** (#W5352—$1.50)

☐ **ELEANOR AND FRANKLIN by Joseph P. Lash.** Foreword by Arthur M. Schlesinger, Jr. A number 1 bestseller and winner of the Pulitzer Prize and the National Book Award, this is the intimate chronicle of Eleanor Roosevelt and her marriage to Franklin D. Roosevelt, with its painful secrets and public triumphs. "An exceptionally candid, exhaustive . . . heartrending book."—**The New Yorker** (#J5310—$1.95)

☐ **JENNIE, VOLUME I: The Life of Lady Randolph Churchill by Ralph G. Martin.** In JENNIE, Ralph G. Martin creates a vivid picture of an exciting woman. Lady Randolph Churchill who was the mother of perhaps the greatest statesman of this century, Winston Churchill, and in her own right, one of the most colorful and fascinating women of the Victorian era. (#E5229—$1.75)

☐ **JENNIE, VOLUME II: The Life of Lady Randolph Churchill, the Dramatic Years 1895-1921 by Ralph G. Martin.** The climactic years of scandalous passion and immortal greatness of the American beauty who raised a son to shape history, Winston Churchill. "An extraordinary lady . . . if you couldn't put down JENNIE ONE, you'll find JENNIE TWO just as compulsive reading!"—**Washington Post** (#E5196—$1.75)

Big Bestsellers from SIGNET

☐ **THURSDAY, MY LOVE by Robert H. Rimmer.** A bold, new novel about open marriage—the biggest future sex shock of all—by the best-selling author of **The Harrad Experiment** and **Proposition 31.** (#Y5237—$1.25)

☐ **WOULD YOU BELIEVE LOVE? by Eliza McCormack.** If there's an over-thirty lady who can read this and not laugh and cry and rage, she'll be hard to find. "Enchanting . . ."—Boston Globe (#Y5197—$1.25)

☐ **TO SMITHEREENS by Rosalyn Drexler.** A heartwarming love story with the kick of a karate chop. . . . "If Lenny Bruce had written a novel, this would have been it!" —Jack Newfield (#Q5281—95¢)

☐ **THE WHITE DAWN by James Houston.** Three white men rescued from a shipwreck by an isolated Eskimo tribe were allowed to live with the natives. This is the story of what happened as two alien cultures moved inexorably on a collision course. . . . "A vivid, boiling adventure of savage excitement and sensual delights . . . powerful and beautiful."—Chicago Sun-Times (#Y5280—$1.25)

☐ **KRUMNAGEL by Peter Ustinov.** KRUMNAGEL asks the all-important question: Can an honest, law-loving, crime-hating police chief overcome the forces of weak-kneed liberalism and stuffy courts of law that want to stop him from using his gun as it was meant to be used—that is to say, every time he feels the urge? "Devastatingly funny!"—Publishers Weekly. "Krumnagel is the anti-hero of the year!"—Harper's (#Y5238—$1.25)
